It's just fun!

– William Dahlgreen, age 5

After having taught literally hundreds of children to read both as a kindergarten teacher and as a certified reading specialist, I was quite picky in going about how I was going to teach my own children to read. I knew I wanted something phonics-based, open-and-go for me as a parent, and mentally and physically engaging for my young children. I knew I did NOT want a million pieces or parts and books to juggle, and I did not want anything I was going to wind up having to supplement with other pieces, parts, and programs. I found what I really wanted in Logic of English *Foundations. Foundations* fully integrates handwriting, phonics, beginning reading, and beginning spelling. There is no need to supplement with other programs. The teacher's manual is well-designed. I didn't need to read through a ton of script to figure out what I was doing that particular day. It has a nice layout. Those parents who really want their hands held in HOW to teach reading will find comfort in this program because everything is there. The activities for the children are fully engaging and can be used as easily with Little Miss Sits Still as well as Mr. Rolls-Around-on-the-Floor. I wish I had Logic of English *Foundations* when I had a classroom of children! But I will settle on using it with my own, knowing that I have seen and tried many programs with many children, and I feel this is absolutely the best program available.

– Lori Archer, M.Ed., Reading Specialist, Homeschool Teacher

The progress in my son's reading and writing abilities in the few months since we began using *Foundations* is truly unbelievable. My son has gone from a very reluctant, struggling reader, to a confident and happy learner. The lessons are well-paced, engaging, and so full of activities and fun that he doesn't notice how much he is learning – but I do.

– Elisa St. Clair, Homeschool Teacher

I have been able to teach my 6th grade dyslexic child, my 4th grade strong reader and my 2nd grade emerging reader all at the same time, and actually enjoy it!

– Kyle Snead Thomas, Homeschool Teacher

Today while playing a reading game my son was giggling and said, "This is awesome!" LOE *Foundations* has made teaching easy and fun. I wish I'd had this program when teaching my other kids!

– Jonie Arends, Homeschool Teacher

This program not only taught my active child to read and write; *Foundations* taught me to work with my active child's natural energy level and interests. Learning together is fun again!

– Heather Aliano, Homeschool Teacher

Today my 5 year old daughter said, "Mom, I love English, you make everything fun!" I cannot put in words how grateful I am for Logic of English. English is not my native tongue and we've struggled with English until we switched to LOE. Now my 5- and 6-year-old daughters plead for LOE. Why not? It is fun (even for me)! Not only is it a program with well laid out instructions for the teacher, it uses all styles of learning so no matter the abilities of the student they will learn.

– Adriana B., Homeschool Mom

I am so thankful to have discovered Logic of English. Teaching my oldest reading was becoming more and more challenging each day. Starting *Foundations* has really changed that for us, and as a bonus my younger daughter was interested, so she has joined in on our teaching time. The program is well laid out and enjoyable to use. Thank you for making me excited to teach English instead of dreading it each day.

– Rachel Walters, Homeschooler

Being new to homeschooling and having struggled with English as a student, I was apprehensive about teaching our children to read. When I came across LOE I knew why I had struggled so much; the phonograms and rules had never been taught to me. As I began to teach my son, not only did he soak up everything, but I found myself learning something new with every lesson. The Logic of English *Foundations* equips parents/teachers with the tools to teach their child how to decode words while making reading fun. Brilliant!

– Erin Stewart, Homeschooling Mom of 3

LOE is a great part of our homeschooling curriculum! It makes learning fun, even for myself as I finally learn why English is the way it is! It should be in every school!

– Trisha Koski

I love learning to write cursive and I love that you get to play games. I love to do school in the morning at our house.

– Bella, age 4

I like the handwriting a lot, because then we can learn cursive. I don't think many 4-year-olds (sister Bella, age 4) and 6-year-olds know cursive. Learning phonograms is fun and you get to do games in it.

– Kaylin, age 6

Foundations

Level A Teacher's Manual

Denise Eide

Logic of English®

Foundations Level A Teacher's Manual by Logic of English

Printed in the United States of America.

Pedia Learning Inc.
10800 Lyndale Ave S. Suite 181
Minneapolis, MN 55420

Cover Design & Illustration: Ingrid Hess
LOE School Font: David Occhino Design

ISBN 978-1-936706-30-3

First Edition

10 9 8 7 6 5 4 3

www.LogicOfEnglish.com

Scope & Sequence

Lesson	Phonemic Awareness	Handwriting	Spelling
1	Develop a kinesthetic awareness of how sounds are formed. Learn that two words can be blended together to form a new word.	Become familiar with lines on paper. Learn the swing stroke.	
2	Develop a kinesthetic awareness of how sounds are formed. Practice blending two words into one word.	Learn the down stroke Review the lines and the swing stroke.	
3	Practice distinguishing sounds from one another. Learn to auditorily blend sounds into words.	Learn the roll stroke.	
4	Listen for /th/ and /TH/. Practice blending words together.	Learn the curve stroke or the straight stroke.	
5	Compare the sounds /s/, /z/, and /th/. Distinguish sounds in isolation. Practice blending sounds into words.	Learn the phonogram a.	
Review Lesson A			
6	Distinguish sounds in isolation. Practice blending sounds into words.	Learn the phonogram d.	
7	Listen for sounds at the beginning of words. Practice blending sounds into words.	Learn the drop-swoop stroke.	
8	Listen for sounds at the beginning of words. Practice blending sounds into words.	Learn the phonogram g.	
9	Listen for sounds at the beginning of words. Practice blending sounds into words.	Learn the phonogram c.	
10	Practice blending sounds into words. Learn to segment words into sounds.	Learn the phonogram o.	
Review Lesson B			
11	Practice listening for sounds at the beginning of words. Practice blending consonants. Practice segmenting words.	Learn the drop-hook stroke.	
12	Practice listening for sounds at the beginning of words. Practice blending consonants. Practice segmenting words.	Learn the phonogram qu.	

Lesson	Phonemic Awareness	Handwriting	Spelling
13	Learn how to sort vowels and consonants. Practice blending consonants. Practice segmenting words into sounds.	Learn the scoop or curve stroke.	
14	Review the difference between consonants and vowels. Practice blending consonants. Practice distinguishing vowel sounds in isolation.	Learn the phonogram s.	
15	Identify phonograms at the beginning of words. Practice blending consonants. Practice distinguishing vowel sounds in isolation.	Learn the cross stroke.	
	Review Lesson C		
16	Practice distinguishing vowel sounds. Review segmenting words.	Learn the phonogram t.	
17	Identify the phonogram at the beginning of the word. Practice blending and segmenting.	Learn the phonogram i.	
18	Practice identifying phonograms at the beginning of the word. Practice blending words together.	Learn the circle stroke.	
19	Identify the phonogram at the beginning of the word.	Learn the phonogram p.	
20	Practice listening for sounds at the end of the word.	Learn the phonogram u.	
	Review Lesson D		
21	Practice listening for sounds at the end of the word.	Learn the phonogram j.	cat, dad, sad, sit, dug
22	Learn to identify the phonogram at the end of the word.	Learn the phonogram w.	up, pig, pup, sat, it
23	Practice identifying the phonogram at the end of the word.	Learn to connect phonograms with the dip stroke (cursive only).	dog, cop, top, pot, pop
24	Practice identifying phonograms at the end of the word.	Learn the bump stroke.	jug, dig, cup, tap, dip
25	Practice identifying phonograms at the end of words. Practice consonant blends.	Learn the phonogram r.	rat, jog, wig, rip, pat
	Review Lesson E		
26	Identify the vowel sound heard in the middle of the word. Practice consonant blends.	Learn the phonogram n.	can, and, quit, nut, nap

Lesson	Phonemic Awareness	Handwriting	Spelling
27	Practice identifying vowels heard in the middle of words. Practice consonant blends.	Learn the phonogram m. Learn to leave a space between words.	Learn about spaces between words.
28	Practice identifying vowels heard in the middle of the word. Practice consonant blends.	Learn the loop stroke or slant stroke.	map, man, mom, gum, tan
29	Identify vowel sounds heard in the middle of the word. Practice consonant blends.	Learn the phonogram e.	pen, jet, pet, net, wet
30	Listen for vowels. Practice consonant blends.	Learn the phonogram l.	quilt, log, men, mad, leg
Review Lesson F			
31	Match the initial sounds of words to the phonogram. Practice blends.	Learn the phonogram b.	big, sand, ran, bad, bend
32	Identify the beginning sound and match it to the phonogram. Practice blends.	Learn the phonogram h.	red, bat, hit, dot, band
33	Create new words by changing the first sound. Practice blends.	Learn the phonogram k.	sink, honk, skunk, ink, link
34	Create new words by changing the first sound.	Learn the phonogram f.	fast, nest, list, best, last
35	Blend multi-syllable words.	Learn the phonogram v.	van, vest, kid, win, rest
Review Lesson G			
36	Learn about short vowel sounds and how to mark them.	Learn the phonogram x.	box, milk, tent, wax, fist
37	Review the short vowel sounds.	Learn the phonogram y.	yes, jump, six, skin, skip
38	Learn about long vowel sounds.	Learn the phonogram z.	if, zip, fox, flag, flap
39	Review short and long vowel sounds.		bed, sun, wind, stomp, stamp
40	Celebration Day!		
Review Lesson H			

Foundations

Equipping teachers to combine the art of teaching with the science of reading!

Supplies Needed

At the beginning of each lesson, *Foundations* includes a list of needed and optional materials. The materials needed for each activity are listed in a box near the beginning of each activity, with optional materials written in italics. It is recommended that the teacher look through each lesson in advance in order to gather the necessary materials. Many lessons include items commonly found in a classroom or home, such as blocks, a mirror, toy cars, stuffed animals, and chalk. In addition to these items, the teacher will need the following:

Foundations Teacher's Manual
Foundations Student Workbook - one per student, in either manuscript or cursive
Basic Phonogram Flash Cards
Rhythm of Handwriting Tactile Cards - in either manuscript or cursive
Rhythm of Handwriting Quick Reference - in either manuscript or cursive
Phonogram Game Cards - two contrasting sets per four students
Phonogram Game Tiles
Doodling Dragons: An ABC Book of Sounds
LOE Student Whiteboard - one per student
Whiteboard markers and eraser
Crayons, glue, scissors

Optional:
Phonics with Phonograms App by Logic of English - available at iTunes
Doodling Dragons App by Logic of English - available at iTunes and Google Play

Cursive or Manuscript?

Foundations includes instructions on how to teach both cursive and manuscript handwriting. Before beginning, the teacher should decide which form of handwriting is best for the student. We suggest all teachers read the article "Why Teach Cursive First?" at http://www.logicofenglish.com/blog/item/238-why-teach-cursive-first. We also suggest teachers consider the following three questions.

Does the student struggle with fine motor activities?

If the student struggles with fine motor skills, it is best to begin with cursive. Cursive handwriting requires significantly less fine motor movement than manuscript. The pencil does not need to be lifted up and down between letters, and placing the pencil to begin each letter is greatly simplified by the fact that all cursive letters begin on the baseline, whereas manuscript letters begin in eight different places.

Does the student show signs of reversing letters while reading and/or writing?

If the student has demonstrated confusion about the direction of b's and d's and p's and q's, cursive can be very helpful in minimizing the issue. Cursive handwriting naturally emphasizes the direction of reading and writing. Furthermore, it is difficult to reverse b's and d's and p's and q's in cursive.

Does the student attend school where manuscript handwriting is taught?

If a parent or tutor is using *Foundations* to supplement a reading program at school, we suggest matching the handwriting style to that of the school to minimize confusion.

Review Lessons

Following every fifth lesson in *Foundations* is a review and assessment lesson. These lessons provide an opportunity to assess the progress of each student and create a custom lesson to address their needs. At this stage all students should be taught to the point of mastery. Assessments should not be used to grade the student, but rather to provide information on which skills need further practice.

Each review lesson includes a chart with the skills which have been taught in the previous ten lessons. Skills marked with a 1 should be mastered before the student progresses to the next lesson. Skills marked with a 2 should be familiar to the child, but the child can still be working towards mastery. Level 2 skills will be practiced extensively in the upcoming lessons, which will provide the student an opportunity to move towards mastery. Skills with a 3 do not need to be mastered in order for students to progress. Some activities labeled with a 3 are beneficial to some students, but not necessary for all students. Other Level 3 skills will be covered extensively in later lessons. Level 3 skills are listed in the chart; however, they are not included in the assessment activities.

Speech Tips

Some lessons include tips for helping students to clearly articulate a sound(s). For further ideas we recommend the resource *Eliciting Sounds: Techniques and Strategies for Clinicians 2nd Edition*, by Wayne A. Secord, Cengage Learning 2007.

Terms

Phonogram - A visual representation of a sound. A phonogram may have one, two, three, or four letters (p**e**n, r**ai**n, n**igh**t, d**augh**ter). *Foundations A* teaches students 25 single-letter phonograms and their sounds, as well as one two-letter phonogram: qu.

CVC Word - A word that follows the pattern: consonant-vowel-consonant.

Pronunciation - Letters that are between two slashes should be referred to by the sound(s). For example, /k/ indicates the sound /k/, not the letter name "kay."

Phonograms

a	/ă-ā-ä/	m***a***t	t***a***ble	f***a***ther	
b	/b/	***b***at			
c	/k-s/	***c***at	***c***ent		
d	/d/	***d***ad			
e	/ĕ-ē/	t***e***nt	b***e***		
f	/f/	***f***oot			
g	/g-j/	bi***g***	***g***ym		
h	/h/	***h***at			
i	/ĭ-ī-ē-y/	***i***t	***i***vy	stad***i***um	on***i***on
j	/j/	***j***ob			
k	/k/	***k***it			
l	/l/	***l***ap			
m	/m/	***m***e			
n	/n/	***n***ut			
o	/ŏ-ō-ö/	***o***n	g***o***	d***o***	
p	/p/	***p***an			
qu	/kw/	***qu***een			
r	/r/	***r***an			
s	/s-z/	***s***ent	a***s***		
t	/t/	***t***ip			
u	/ŭ-ū-oo-ü/	***u***p	p***u***pil	fl***u***te	p***u***t
v	/v/	***v***an			
w	/w/	***w***all			
x	/ks-z/	fo***x***	***x***ylophone		
y	/y-ĭ-ī-ē/	***y***ard	g***y***m	b***y***	bab***y***
z	/z/	***z***ip			

Materials Needed

Lesson	Materials Needed	Optional
1	LOE whiteboard, Tactile Card or	Mirror, Dr. Seuss book, table, statue with a base
2	LOE whiteboard, blue, green, and red whiteboard markers, Tactile Cards or	Dr. Seuss book, LEGO®s, toy car
3	LOE whiteboard, Tactile Card or	Dr. Seuss book, a collection of toy animals, ball
4	LOE whiteboard, red, black, and blue whiteboard markers, all the Tactile Cards learned so far and or	Dr. Seuss book, dress-up clothes, blender, frozen fruit, juice, candy bar with segments, picture of an ant, shaving cream and tray
5	LOE whiteboard, timer, a children's book, Phonogram Card a, Tactile Card a or a, *Doodling Dragons: An ABC Book of Sounds*	Dr. Seuss book, foods and activities for "a" Day
A Review	Ball, basket or box, LOE Whiteboard, red, black, and blue whiteboard markers	Eight LEGO®s or blocks per student
6	LOE whiteboard, crayons, Phonogram Cards a and d, *Doodling Dragons*, Tactile Card d or d, sensory box with salt or cornmeal	Foods and activities for "d" Day
7	Two LOE whiteboards, crayons or markers, Phonogram Cards a and d, Tactile Card or, crackers or pennies to keep score, timer	Stickers
8	LOE whiteboard, Phonogram Cards a, d, g, *Doodling Dragons*, Tactile Card g or g, sensory box	Foods and activities for "g" Day, sidewalk chalk or sheets of paper
9	LOE whiteboard, Phonogram Cards learned so far and c, Tactile Card c or c, *Doodling Dragons*, sidewalk chalk, bean bag, paper plates, markers or crayons	Foods and activities for "c" Day, stamp and ink
10	LOE whiteboard, *Doodling Dragons*, Phonogram Cards learned so far and o, Tactile Card o or o	Rhythm of Handwriting Quick Reference, foods and activities for "o" Day, balance beam or masking tape
B Review	Phonogram Cards a, c, d, g, o, red, blue, yellow, black, and green crayons, highlighter, LOE whiteboard or sensory box	Fly swatter or toy sticky hand, shaving cream

Lesson	Materials Needed	Optional
11	LOE whiteboard and colored markers, Phonogram Cards, Tactile Card [f] or [f], index cards	Toy animals, sidewalk chalk, Tactile Cards or Sandpaper Letters
12	LOE whiteboard, Phonogram Card [qu], Tactile Card [qu] or [qu], 1-2 sets of Phonogram Game Cards, *Doodling Dragons*, playdough, popsicle sticks	Activities for "qu" Day
13	LOE whiteboard, Phonogram Cards, Tactile Card [illegible] or [illegible], whipped cream, plastic plate	Phonogram Game Cards
14	LOE whiteboard, Phonogram Card [s], two sets of Phonogram Game Cards, Tactile Card [s] or [s], *Doodling Dragons*, sidewalk chalk, ball	Mirror, Rhythm of Handwriting Quick Reference, foods, books, and activities for "s" Day, paper, markers
15	LOE whiteboard, Phonogram Cards, crackers or chocolate pieces to keep score, Rhythm of Handwriting Quick Reference or [illegible]	Phonogram Game Cards
C **Review**	Red, blue, yellow, black, and green crayons, ball, basket, highlighter, Phonogram Cards, NERF® gun or ball	LOE whiteboard or sensory box, ball and bowling pins or target
16	LOE whiteboard, Phonogram Card [t], Tactile Card [t] or [t], *Doodling Dragons*, large whiteboard, NERF® gun with suction cup darts or soft ball	Foods, books, and activities for "t" Day, flashlight, index cards, tape, Sandpaper Letters
17	LOE whiteboard, all the Phonogram Cards learned so far and [i], crayons, *Doodling Dragons*, Tactile Card [i] or [i], chocolate chips or tokens for a Bingo game, ball, index cards, playdough, alphabet cookie cutters	Foods, books, and activities for "i" Day, Phonogram Game Cards
18	LOE whiteboard, markers, Phonogram Cards, Tactile Card [illegible] or [illegible], obstacles for an obstacle course	Blank paper and clipboard, fly swatter or sticky hand toy
19	LOE whiteboard, Phonogram Card [p], Tactile Card [p] or [p], *Doodling Dragons*, pennies or tokens for a Bingo game, Phonogram Game Cards, stop watch	Foods, books, and activities for "p" Day
20	LOE whiteboard, Phonogram Card [u], Tactile Card [u] or [u], two sets of Phonogram Game Cards, *Doodling Dragons*, sensory box with salt, whipped cream, or shaving cream	Foods, books, and activities for "u" Day
D **Review**	Phonogram cards, green and brown crayons, ball, basket, highlighter	LOE whiteboard or sensory box

Lesson	Materials Needed	Optional
21	LOE whiteboard, all the Phonogram Cards learned so far and j, Tactile Card j or j, *Doodling Dragons*	Foods, books, and activities for "j" Day, Phonogram Game Tiles, 2 sets of Phonogram Game Cards
22	LOE whiteboard, Phonogram Game Cards, Phonogram Card w, Tactile Card w or w, *Doodling Dragons*, timer	Foods, books, and activities for "w" Day, blocks, playdough, alphabet cookie cutters, Phonogram Game Tiles
23	LOE whiteboard, Phonogram Cards, 2 sets of Phonogram Game Cards, Phonogram Game Tiles	Sensory tray with shaving cream, whipped cream, or pudding, Rhythm of Handwriting Quick Reference, toy top, picture of a top hat
24	LOE whiteboard, Phonogram Cards, Tactile Card r or r, sensory box with salt, sand, or cornmeal, timer, blocks or LEGO®s	Die, Phonogram Game Tiles, jug with water, cups, carrots and dip
25	LOE whiteboard, Phonogram Cards p, s, t, r, Tactile Card r or r, *Doodling Dragons*, two sets of Phonogram Game Cards, cloth bag, timer, scissors, glue, Reader 1	Wig, foods, books, and activities for "r" Day, Phonogram Game Tiles, crayons, two or three sheets of paper
E Review	Ball, basket, Phonogram Cards, highlighter	Tactile Cards, whiteboard, sensory box
26	LOE whiteboard, all the Phonogram Cards learned so far and n, Tactile Card n or n, *Doodling Dragons*, crayons, markers, or colored pencils, glue, scissors	Foods, books, and activities for "n" Day, Tactile Card n, two sets of Phonogram Game Cards, cloth bag, timer, Phonogram Game Tiles, finger paint and paper, can and can opener, objects for plural practice, index cards
27	LOE whiteboard, all the Phonogram Cards learned so far and m, Tactile Card m or m, Phonogram Game Cards, *Doodling Dragons*, Bingo tokens, highlighter	Foods, books, and activities for "m" Day
28	LOE whiteboard, Phonogram Cards, Tactile Card z or z, two sets of Phonogram Game Cards, scissors, glue, Reader 2	Phonogram Game Tiles, pudding
29	LOE whiteboard, all the Phonogram Cards learned so far and e, Tactile Card e or e, *Doodling Dragons*, timer, Phonogram Game Cards, scissors, hat or basket	Foods, books, and activities for "e" Day, Phonogram Game Tiles, two colors of tempera paint in a gallon-size ziplock bag
30	LOE whiteboard, Phonogram Cards t and l, Tactile Card l or l, *Doodling Dragons*, timer, Phonogram Game Cards, large whiteboard and colored markers, glue, scissors, Reader 3	Sidewalk chalk or finger paints and large pieces of paper, foods and activities for "l" Day, music, Phonogram Game Tiles, *The Keeping Quilt* by Patricia Polacco
F Review	Phonogram Cards, highlighter	Sensory box or whiteboard

Lesson	Materials Needed	Optional
31	3-5 LOE whiteboards, Phonogram Cards b, n, d, Tactile Card b or b, *Doodling Dragons*, box or basket, scissors	Foods, books, and activities for "b" Day, Phonogram Game Tiles, squirt guns, chalkboard, finger paint and paper
32	LOE whiteboard, Phonogram Card h, Tactile Card h or h, Phonogram Game Cards, *Doodling Dragons*, scissors, glue, Reader 4	Foods, books, and activities for "h" Day, timer, Sandpaper Letters, Phonogram Game Tiles, chalkboard and chalk
33	LOE whiteboard, all the Phonogram Cards learned so far and k, Tactile Card k or k, Phonogram Game Tiles, *Doodling Dragons*, game pieces, scissors	Foods, books, and activities for "k" Day, rope for a kangaroo tail, Rhythm of Handwriting Quick Reference or [illegible]
34	LOE whiteboard, Phonogram Cards f, s, t, Tactile Card f or f, Phonogram Game Tiles, *Doodling Dragons*, game pieces, scissors	Foods, books, and activities for "f" Day, mirror, window paint
35	LOE whiteboard, Phonogram Card v, Tactile Card v or v, *Doodling Dragons*, two sets of Phonogram Game Cards, hat or basket, scissors, glue, Reader 5	Foods, books and activities for "v" Day, Phonogram Game Tiles, Rhythm of Handwriting Quick Reference
G Review	Highlighter, Phonogram Cards	LOE whiteboard, sensory box
36	LOE whiteboard, all the Phonogram Cards learned so far and x, Tactile Cards z or z and x or x, *Doodling Dragons*, bell or buzzer, scissors	Foods, books, and activities for "x" Day, Phonogram Game Tiles, obstacles
37	LOE whiteboard, Phonogram Card y, Tactile Card y or y, *Doodling Dragons*, two sets of Phonogram Game Cards, scissors	Foods, books, and activities for "y" Day, Phonogram Game Tiles
38	LOE whiteboard, Phonogram Cards a, e, i, o, u, z, Tactile Card z or z, *Doodling Dragons*, game pieces, die, scissors	Foods, books, and activities for "y" Day, Phonogram Game Tiles
39	LOE whiteboard, Phonogram Cards, Bingo tokens, obstacles for the obstacle course, scissors, glue, Reader 6	Phonogram Game Tiles, clipboards, blank paper
40	Foods, games, crafts, and activities for an alphabet party	
H Review	Highlighter, Phonogram Cards	LOE whiteboard, sensory box

Common Core Standards

Standard		Foundations Lesson A, B, & C
Kindergarten Reading Foundational Skills		
RF.K.1a	Follow words from left to right, top to bottom, and page by page.	21-120
RF.K.1b	Recognize that spoken words are represented in written language by specific sequences of letters.	21-120
RF.K.1c	Understand that words are separated by spaces in print.	27-120
RF.K.1d	Recognize and name all upper- and lowercase letters of the alphabet.	5-68
RF.K.2a	Recognize and produce rhyming words.	64-65, 70, 76, 78-79
RF.K.2b	Count, pronounce, blend, and segment syllables in spoken words.	42-44, 51-52, 75, 82-120
RF.K.2c	Blend and segment onsets and rimes of single-syllable spoken words.	3-10
RF.K.2d	Isolate and pronounce the initial, medial vowel, and final sounds (phonemes) in three-phoneme (consonant-vowel-consonant, or CVC) words.	7-9, 11-12, 15, 17-29, 31-32
RF.K.2e	Add or substitute individual sounds (phonemes) in simple, one-syllable words to make new words.	33-34, 46-47, 60, 80, 91-92, 99, 106
RF.K.3a	Demonstrate basic knowledge of one-to-one letter-sound correspondences by producing the primary sound or many of the most frequent sounds for each consonant.	6-40
RF.K.3b	Associate the long and short sounds with the common spellings (graphemes) for the five major vowels.	5-40
RF.K.3c	Read common high-frequency words by sight (e.g. the, of, to, you, she, my, is, are, do, does).	42-120
RF.K.3d	Distinguish between similarly spelled words by identifying the sounds of the letters that differ.	77
RF.K.4	Read emergent-reader texts with purpose and understanding.	25, 30, 35, 40, 45, 50, 55, 60, 65, 70, 75, 80-84, 86-89, 91-94, 96-99, 101-104, 106-109, 111-113, 116-118
First Grade Reading Foundational Skills		
RF.1.1a	Recognize the distinguishing features of a sentence (e.g. first word, capitalization, ending punctuation).	44, 110
RF.1.2a	Distinguish long from short vowel sounds in spoken single-syllable words.	36-39, 41, 50, 54, 56-59, 61 62, 68-69, 89, 95, 96
RF.1.2b	Orally produce single-syllable words by blending sounds (phonemes), including consonant blends.	3-120 (This skill is practiced through spelling dictation.)
RF.1.2c	Isolate and pronounce initial, medial vowel, and final sounds (phonemes) in spoken single-syllable words.	7-9, 11-12, 15, 17-29, 31-32

Standard		Foundations Lesson A, B, & C
RF.1.2d	Segment spoken single-syllable words into their complete sequence of individual sounds (phonemes).	10-120 (This skill is practiced through spelling dictation.)
RF.1.3a	Know the spelling-sound correspondences for common consonant digraphs.	41-120 (Introduced throughout and practiced daily with phonogram games.)
RF.1.3b	Decode regularly spelled one-syllable words.	21-120
RF.1.3c	Know final -e and common vowel team conventions for representing long vowel sounds.	48-120 (Introduced throughout and practiced daily through phonogram games and silent E games.)
RF.1.3d	Use knowledge that every syllable must have a vowel sound to determine the number of syllables in a printed word.	105
RF.1.3e	Decode two-syllable words following basic patterns by breaking the words into syllables.	81-90, 92-120
RF.1.3f	Read words with inflectional endings.	86-90, 92-94, 98, 101, 111-113
RF.1.3g	Recognize and read grade-appropriate irregularly spelled words.	45, 55, 66-67, 76, 81, 86, 98,100, 102, 108, 110-111, 117
RF.1.4a	Read grade-level text with purpose and understanding.	25, 30, 35, 40, 45, 50, 55, 60, 65, 70, 75, 80, 81-84, 86-89, 91-94, 96-99, 101-104, 106-109
RF.1.4b	Read grade-level text orally with accuracy, appropriate rate, and expression on successive readings.	25, 30, 35, 40, 45, 50, 55, 60, 65, 70, 75, 80, 81-84, 86-89, 91-94, 96-99, 101-104, 106-109
RF.1.4c	Use context to confirm or self-correct word recognition and understanding, rereading as necessary.	80, 81-84, 86-89, 91-94, 96-99, 101-104, 106-109
Kindergarten Language Skills		
L.K.1a	Print many upper- and lowercase letters.	5-68
L.K.1b	Use frequently occurring nouns and verbs.	1-120
L.K.1c	Form regular plural nouns orally by adding /s/ or /es/ (e.g. dog, dogs; wish, wishes).	53, 57, 75, 93-94
L.K.1d	Understand and use question words (interrogatives) (e.g. who, what, where, when, why, how).	52, 58, 74, 77
L.K.1e	Use the most frequently occurring prepositions (e.g. to, from, in, out, on, off, for, of, by, with).	24, 47, 49, 54, 59, 62, 64, 69, 71, 72, 73, 78,
L.K.1f	Produce and expand complete sentences in shared language activities.	1-120
L.K.2a	Capitalize the first word in a sentence and the pronoun I.	44, 75, 110
L.K.2b	Recognize and name end punctuation.	44
L.K.2c	Write a letter or letters for most consonant and short-vowel sounds (phonemes).	5-80
L.K.2d	Spell simple words phonetically, drawing on knowledge of sound-letter relationships.	21-120

Standard		Foundations Lesson A, B, & C
L.K.4a	Identify new meanings for familiar words and apply them accurately (e.g. knowing duck is a bird and learning the verb to duck).	1, 23
L.K.4b	Use the most frequently occurring inflections and affixes (e.g. -ed, -s, re-, un-, pre-, -ful, -less) as a clue to the meaning of an unknown word.	53, 86-90, 91-94, 98, 101-103, 108, 111-113, 116
L.K.5a	Sort common objects into categories (e.g. shapes, foods) to gain a sense of the concepts the categories represent.	99
L.K.5b	Demonstrate understanding of frequently occurring verbs and adjectives by relating them to their opposites (antonyms).	113
L.K.5c	Identify real-life connections between words and their use (e.g. note places at school that are colorful).	82-83, 87-88, 92-93, 97-98, 102-103, 108-109, 112-113, 118-119
L.K.5d	Distinguish shades of meaning among verbs describing the same general action (e.g. walk, march, strut, prance) by acting out the meanings.	6, 7
L.K.6	Use words and phrases acquired through conversations, reading and being read to, and responding to texts.	82-83, 87-88, 92-93, 97-98, 102-103, 108-109, 112-113, 118-119
Kindergarten Reading Literature		
RL.K.1	With prompting and support, ask and answer questions about key details in a text.	45, 50, 55, 60, 65, 70, 75, 80
RL.K.2	With prompting and support, retell familiar stories, including key details.	45, 50, 55, 60, 65, 70, 75, 80
RL.K.3	With prompting and support, identify characters, settings, and major events in a story.	45, 50, 55, 60, 65, 70, 75, 80
RL.K.4	Ask and answer questions about unknown words in a text.	45, 50, 55, 60, 65, 70, 75, 80
RI.K.5	Recognize common types of texts (e.g. storybooks, poems).	114
RI.K.6	With prompting and support, name the author and illustrator of a story and define the role of each in telling the story.	45, 50, 55, 60, 65, 70, 75, 80
RI.K.7	With prompting and support, describe the relationship between illustrations and the story in which they appear (e.g. what moment in a story an illustration depicts).	60, 75
RI.K.9	With prompting and support, compare and contrast the adventures and experiences of characters in familiar stories.	55
RL.K.10	Actively engage in group reading activities with purpose and understanding.	45, 50, 55, 60, 65, 70, 75, 80
Kindergarten Reading Informational Texts		
RI.K.1	With prompting and support, ask and answer questions about key details in a text.	83, 88, 93, 98, 103, 109, 113, 119

Standard		Foundations Lesson A, B, & C
RI.K.2	With prompting and support, identify the main topic and retell key details of a text.	90, 96, 104, 106, 108-110
RI.K.3	With prompting and support, describe the connection between two individuals, events, ideas, or pieces of information in a text.	83, 88, 93, 98, 103, 109, 113, 119
RI.K.4	With prompting and support, ask and answer questions about unknown words in a text.	83, 88, 93, 98, 103, 109, 113, 119
RI.K.5	Identify the front cover, back cover, and title page of a book.	83, 88
RI.K.6	Name the author and illustrator of a text and define the role of each in presenting the ideas or information in a text.	82, 87
RI.K.7	With prompting and support, describe the relationship between illustrations and the text in which they appear.	83, 88, 93, 98, 103, 109, 113, 119
RI.K.8	With prompting and support, identify the reasons an author gives to support points in a text.	83, 88, 93, 98, 103, 109, 113, 119
RI.K.9	With prompting and support, identify basic similarities in and differences between two texts on the same topic.	Foundations D-F
RI.K.10	Actively engage in group reading activities with purpose and understanding.	83, 88, 93, 98, 103, 109, 113, 119
Kindergarten Writing		
W.K.1	Use a combination of drawing, dictating, and writing to compose opinion pieces in which they tell a reader the topic or the name of the book they are writing about and state an opinion or preference about the topic or book (e.g., My favorite book is...).	95
W.K.2	Use a combination of drawing, dictating, and writing to compose informative/explanatory texts in which they name what they are writing about and supply some information about the topic.	49, 85, 90, 95, 100, 105, 110, 114, 115, 119, 120
W.K.3	Use a combination of drawing, dictating, and writing to narrate a single event or several loosely linked events, tell about the events in the order in which they occurred, and provide a reaction to what happened.	49, 64, 69, 72, 78, 89, 115
W.K.5	With guidance and support from adults, respond to questions and suggestions from peers and add details to strengthen writing as needed.	85, 90, 95, 100, 105, 110, 114, 115, 119, 120
W.K.6	With guidance and support from adults, explore a variety of digital tools to produce and publish writing, including in collaboration with peers.	Foundations D-F
W.K.7	Participate in shared research and writing projects (e.g. explore a number of books by a favorite author and express opinions about them).	Foundations D-F
W.K.8	With guidance and support from adults, recall information from experiences or gather information from provided sources to answer a question.	Foundations D-F

Common Core Standards

Lesson	Standards
1	RF.K.2c, RF.1.2b
2	RF.K.2c, RF.1.2b
3	RF.K.2c, RF.1.2b
4	RF.K.2c, RF.1.2b
5	RF.K.1b, RF.K.2c, RF.K.3b, L.K.2c, L.1.1a, RF.1.2b
6	RF.K.3b, L.K.5d, L.K.2c, L.1.1a, RF.1.2b
7	RF.K.2c, RF.K.2d, RF.K.3a, RF.K.3b, L.K.5d, RF.1.2b
8	RF.K.2c, RF.K.2d, RF.K.3a, RF.K.3b, L.K.2c, L.1.1a, RF.1.2b
9	RF.K.2c, RF.K.2d, RF.K.3a, RF.K.3b, L.K.2c, L.1.1a, RF.1.2b
10	RF.K.2c, RF.K.2d, RF.K.3a, RF.K.3b, L.K.2c, L.1.1a, RF.1.2b
11	RF.K.1d, RF.K.2b, RF.K.2d, RF.K.3a, RF.1.2b, RF.1.2c, RF.1.2d, L.K.2c, L.1.1a
12	RF.K.1d, RF.K.2b, RF.K.2d, RF.K.3a, RF.1.2b, RF.1.2c, RF.1.2d, L.K.2c, L.1.1a
13	RF.K.1d, RF.K.2b, RF.K.2d, RF.K.3a, RF.1.2b, RF.1.2c, RF.1.2d, L.K.2c, L.1.1a
14	RF.K.1d, RF.K.2b, RF.K.2d, RF.K.3a, RF.1.2b, RF.1.2c, RF.1.2d, L.K.2c, L.1.1a
15	RF.K.1d, RF.K.2b, RF.K.2d, RF.K.3a, RF.1.2b, RF.1.2c, RF.1.2d, L.K.2c, L.1.1a
16	RF.K.1d, RF.K.2b, RF.K.2d, RF.K.3a, RF.1.2b, RF.1.2c, RF.1.2d, L.K.2c, L.1.1a
17	RF.K.1d, RF.K.2b, RF.K.2d, RF.K.3a, RF.1.2b, RF.1.2c, RF.1.2d, L.K.2c, L.1.1a
18	RF.K.1d, RF.K.2b, RF.K.2d, RF.K.3a, RF.1.2b, RF.1.2c, RF.1.2d, L.K.2c, L.1.1a
19	RF.K.1d, RF.K.2b, RF.K.2d, RF.K.3a, RF.1.2b, RF.1.2c, RF.1.2d, L.K.2c, L.1.1a
20	RF.K.1d, RF.K.2b, RF.K.2d, RF.K.3a, RF.1.2b, RF.1.2c, RF.1.2d, L.K.2c, L.1.1a

Lesson	Standards
21	RF.K.1a, RF.K.1b, RF.K.1d, RF.K.2b, RF.K.2c, RF.K.2d, RF.K.3a, RF.K.3b, RF.K.3d, RF.1.2b, RF.1.2c, RF.1.2d, RF.1.3d, L.K.1a, L.K.2c, L.K.2d, L.1.1a, L.1.2e
22	RF.K.1a, RF.K.1b, RF.K.1d, RF.K.2b, RF.K.2c, RF.K.2d, RF.K.3a, RF.K.3b, RF.K.3d, RF.1.2b, RF.1.2c, RF.1.2d, RF.1.3d, L.K.1a, L.K.2c, L.K.2d, L.1.1a, L.1.2e
23	RF.K.1a, RF.K.1b, RF.K.1d, RF.K.2b, RF.K.2c, RF.K.2d, RF.K.3a, RF.K.3b, RF.K.3d, RF.1.2b, RF.1.2c, RF.1.2d, RF.1.3d, L.K.1a, L.K.2c, L.K.2d, L.1.1a, L.1.2e
24	RF.K.1a, RF.K.1b, RF.K.1d, RF.K.2b, RF.K.2c, RF.K.2d, RF.K.3a, RF.K.3b, RF.K.3d, RF.1.2b, RF.1.2c, RF.1.2d, RF.1.3d, L.K.1a, L.K.2c, L.K.2d, L.1.1a, L.1.2e
25	RF.K.1a, RF.K.1b, RF.K.1d, RF.K.2b, RF.K.2c, RF.K.2d, RF.K.3a, RF.K.3b, RF.K.3d, RF.1.2b, RF.1.2c, RF.1.2d, RF.1.3d, L.K.1a, L.K.2c, L.K.2d, L.1.1a, L.1.2e, SL.K.5
26	RF.K.1a, RF.K.1b, RF.K.1d, RF.K.2b, RF.K.2c, RF.K.2d, RF.K.3a, RF.K.3b, RF.K.3d, RF.1.2b, RF.1.2c, RF.1.2d, RF.1.3d, RF.1.3f L.K.1a, L.K.2c, L.K.2d, L.1.1a, L.1.2e
27	RF.K.1a, RF.K.1b, RF.K.1d, RF.K.2b, RF.K.2c, RF.K.2d, RF.K.3a, RF.K.3b, RF.K.3d, RF.1.2b, RF.1.2c, RF.1.2d, RF.1.3d, L.K.1a, L.K.2c, L.K.2d, L.1.1a, L.1.2e
28	RF.K.1a, RF.K.1b, RF.K.1d, RF.K.2b, RF.K.2c, RF.K.2d, RF.K.3a, RF.K.3b, RF.K.3d, RF.1.2b, RF.1.2c, RF.1.2d, RF.1.3d, L.K.1a, L.K.2c, L.K.2d, L.1.1a, L.1.2e, SL.K.5
29	RF.K.1a, RF.K.1b, RF.K.1d, RF.K.2b, RF.K.2c, RF.K.2d, RF.K.3a, RF.K.3b, RF.K.3d, RF.1.2b, RF.1.2c, RF.1.2d, RF.1.3d, L.K.1a, L.K.2c, L.K.2d, L.1.1a, L.1.2e
30	RF.K.1a, RF.K.1b, RF.K.1d, RF.K.2b, RF.K.2c, RF.K.2d, RF.K.3a, RF.K.3b, RF.K.3d, RF.1.2b, RF.1.2c, RF.1.2d, RF.1.3d, L.K.1a, L.K.2c, L.K.2d, L.1.1a, L.1.2e, SL.K.5
31	RF.K.1a, RF.K.1b, RF.K.1c, RF.K.1d, RF.K.2b, RF.K.2d, RF.K.3a, RF.1.2b, RF.1.2c, RF.1.2d, RF.1.3b, L.K.1a, L.K.2c, L.K.2d, L.1.1a, L.1.2e
32	RF.K.1a, RF.K.1b, RF.K.1c, RF.K.1d, RF.K.2b, RF.K.2d, RF.K.3a, RF.1.2b, RF.1.2c, RF.1.2d, RF.1.3b, L.K.1a, L.K.2c, L.K.2d, L.K.4a, L.1.1a, L.1.2e, SL.K.5
33	RF.K.1a, RF.K.1b, RF.K.1c, RF.K.1d, RF.K.2b, RF.K.2d, RF.K.3a, RF.1.2b, RF.1.2c, RF.1.2d, RF.1.3b, L.K.1a, L.K.2c, L.K.2d, L.K.4a, L.1.1a, L.1.2e
34	RF.K.1a, RF.K.1b, RF.K.1c, RF.K.1d, RF.K.2b, RF.K.2d, RF.K.2e, RF.K.3a, RF.1.2b, RF.1.2c, RF.1.2d, RF.1.3b, L.K.1a, L.K.2c, L.K.2d, L.1.1a, L.1.2e
35	RF.K.1a, RF.K.1b, RF.K.1c, RF.K.1d, RF.K.2b, RF.K.2d, RF.K.3a, RF.1.2b, RF.1.2c, RF.1.2d, RF.1.3b, L.K.1a, L.K.2c, L.K.2d, L.1.1a, L.1.2e, SL.K.5
36	RF.K.1a, RF.K.1b, RF.K.1c, RF.K.1d, RF.K.2b, RF.K.2d, RF.K.3a, RF.K.3b, RF.K.3d, RF.1.2b, RF.1.2c, RF.1.2d, RF.1.3b, L.K.1a, L.K.2c, L.K.2d, L.1.1a, L.1.2e
37	RF.K.1a, RF.K.1b, RF.K.1c, RF.K.1d, RF.K.2b, RF.K.2d, RF.K.3a, RF.K.3d, RF.1.2b, RF.1.2c, RF.1.2d, RF.1.3b, L.K.1a, L.K.2c, L.K.2d, L.K.5d, L.1.1a, L.1.2e, L.1.5d, L.1.1f
38	RF.K.1a, RF.K.1b, RF.K.1c, RF.K.1d, RF.K.2b, RF.K.2d, RF.K.3a, RF.K.3b, RF.K.3d, RF.1.2a, RF.1.2b, RF.1.2c, RF.1.2d, RF.1.3b, L.K.1a, L.K.2c, L.K.2d, L.1.1a, L.1.2e
39	RF.K.1a, RF.K.1b, RF.K.1c, RF.K.1d, RF.K.2b, RF.K.2d, RF.K.3a, RF.1.2b, RF.1.2c, RF.1.2d, RF.1.3b, L.K.1a, L.K.2c, L.K.2d, L.1.1a, L.1.2e, SL.K.5
40	

LESSON 1

Objectives

HANDWRITING: Become familiar with lines on paper. Learn the swing stroke.

PHONEMIC AWARENESS: Develop a kinesthetic awareness of how sounds are formed. Learn that two words can be blended together to form a new word.

Materials

NEEDED: LOE whiteboard, Tactile Card [ ] or [ ] (swing)

OPTIONAL: mirror, Dr. Seuss book, table, statue with a base

Phonemic Awareness

A Kinesthetic Awareness of Sound

Discuss the following questions to help the students begin to think about words.

What is a word? *Answers will vary.*
What are some examples of words?
What makes words different from each other?

Words are made of sounds.
There are 45 sounds that combine together to make English words.
Is 45 a lot of sounds? *Answers will vary.*

One of those sounds is /p/. Say /p/. */p/*
What does your mouth do when you say the sound /p/? *My lips are closed and then pop open.*
Put your hand in front of your mouth as you say /p/. What do you feel as you say the sound? *air popping*
Can you plug your nose and say /p/? *yes*

Now say /b/. How is your mouth shaped when you say /b/? *My lips are closed and then pop open.*

Mirror
Dr. Seuss books

Teacher Tip

By discussing how sounds are formed, students will develop a kinesthetic awareness of sounds. This will provide students with the additional tool of feeling the difference between sounds, not only listening for the difference. This is vital for kinesthetic learners and for students with weak auditory skills.

Multi-Sensory Fun

Have students look in a mirror while forming the sounds. This can be particularly helpful for students with weak auditory skills.

How is it the same as /p/? ***It is exactly the same.***
Can you feel air coming out? ***yes***
Can you plug your nose and say /b/? ***yes***
Why are these sounds different? ***Answers will vary.***

Place your hand on your throat as you say /p/ and /b/. What do you feel? ***My throat buzzes or vibrates when I say /b/ but not /p/.***

Book List

Read a Dr. Seuss book each day this week. Encourage students to listen to how Dr. Seuss plays with sounds.

The place that is vibrating is called your voice box. When you use your voice box to say a sound, it is called a voiced sound. When you do not use your voice box to say the sound, it is called an unvoiced sound. *Un-* means not, so *un*voiced means not voiced.

Place your hand on your throat and say the sound /p/. ***/p/***
Is /p/ voiced or unvoiced? ***unvoiced***
/b/ ***/b/***
Is /b/ voiced or unvoiced? ***voiced***

Multi-Sensory Fun

If a student is struggling to feel the difference between voiced and unvoiced sounds, have her place her hand on your throat to feel the vibrations.

Now say /f/. How do you say /f/? ***I put my top teeth on my bottom lip and blow.***
Put your hand in front of your mouth and feel the air as you say /f/.
Now say /p/ and /f/ and feel the air coming out. How are they different? ***/p/ has a short puff of air and then it stops. For /f/ the air keeps coming out.***

Teacher Tip

Don't be concerned if students do not master the terms: voiced and unvoiced. Rather help them to experience how the sounds are formed.

Now say /v/. How do you say /v/? ***I put my top teeth on my bottom lip and blow.***
Put your hand in front of your mouth and feel the air as you say /v/.
Now say /f/ and /v/. How are they the same? ***My mouth is the same for both of them.***
Place your hand on your throat as you say /f/ and /v/.
How are they different? ***/f/ is unvoiced. /v/ is voiced.***

By putting our mouths in different shapes and turning our voice boxes on and off, we can make different sounds. These sounds make up words.

Compound Words

1.1 Compound Words

On your page you have some pictures. Today we will play a game. I am thinking of a word made of two words that are stuck together. I will say the two words. "Glue" or blend the words together. Shout out the answer and then circle the right picture.

rain	bow	*rainbow*	sail	boat	*sailboat*
foot	ball	*football*	air	plane	*airplane*
pop	corn	*popcorn*	lap	top	*laptop*
back	pack	*backpack*	butter	fly	*butterfly*

Handwriting

Learn the Lines

1.2 Optional Handwriting Chart

Show the LOE Whiteboard with the large lines.

We will use this whiteboard (or chart) to learn how to write our letters.

What do you see on the whiteboard? ***lines, a dotted line***

Point to the baseline.

This is the baseline. Point to the baseline and say its name. ***baseline***

What does the word baseline remind you of? ***baseball, base***

The baseline is where all the letters will sit.

For students beginning with cursive only: The baseline is also the place all the lowercase letters begin.

Point to the top line.

This is the top line.

Point to the top line and say its name. ***top line***

Now point to the baseline and say its name. ***baseline***

Point to the midline.

This is the midline.

Can you think of a word that begins with *mid-*? ***middle, midnight***

Mid- is another way to say middle.

Do you see that the midline is in the middle?

What is the midline between? ***the top line and the baseline***

Point to the top line.

Point to the midline.

Point to the baseline.

Whiteboard

Tactile Card  or 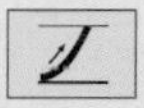 (swing)

Teacher Tip

Handwriting Chart 1.2 may be used as an alternative to the LOE Whiteboard. Slide it into a plastic page protector to be re-used in future lessons. Write on the page protector with wet-erase markers.

Vocabulary

Base - Show students the base of a table or of a statue. Discuss how the table and statue rest on the base. In the same way, the letters will all rest on the baseline.

Teacher Tip

Foundations begins with the handwriting strokes that combine to form letters. Some students and teachers find strokes to be essential for developing good handwriting. They clearly see every letter comprised of the strokes. Others find this confusing. They prefer to learn the letters as a whole. We have found that many students have strong learning style preferences in this area. For students who feel confused by strokes, use these activities to develop muscle control for writing. Beginning in Lesson 5 the strokes will be combined to write phonograms.

Buzz the Teacher

Now you tell me where to point. If I point to the wrong line, say, "buzz." I sometimes get mixed up, so be sure to check me.

Point to the lines as the students call them out. Be sure to get a few wrong so they can "buzz" you.

The Swing Stroke

The lines help us to know where to write the letters. However, before we learn to write letters, we will learn the strokes used to form the letters.

Let's learn our first stroke.

Show the Tactile Card 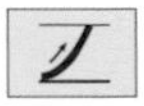 or .

This is called the swing stroke.

What do you notice about the swing stroke? ***It sits on the baseline. It touches the midline.***

Teacher Tip

The directions in green on the left are for cursive; the directions in blue on the right are for manuscript. The strokes are the same for the first three lessons.

Demonstrate how to write the stroke using your pointer finger on the card while saying the directions aloud.

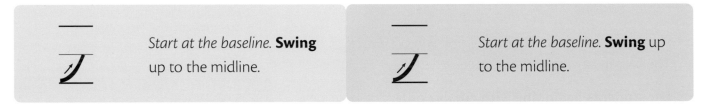

Start at the baseline. **Swing** up to the midline.

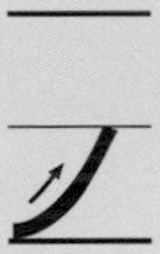

Start at the baseline. **Swing** up to the midline.

Write the swing stroke on the card (or on the whiteboard) with your finger. Say "swing" as you write it. ***swing***
Write the swing stroke in the air. Make it really big. As you write it, say the name of the stroke. ***swing***
Pretend to write the stroke on the ground with your finger. ***swing***
Pretend to write the stroke on your leg with your finger. ***swing***

Teacher Tip

If there are more students than Tactile Cards, ask the students to form the letter with their pointer finger using the large lines on the whiteboard, or use 1.2 Optional Handwriting Chart.

Show the student the whiteboard.

Where would you start to write swing on the whiteboard? ***the baseline***

Point to the baseline.

Write swing with your pointer finger on the whiteboard. ***swing***

Now use a marker and write the swing stroke on the whiteboard.

Multi-Sensory Fun

If your student is a reluctant writer, write the stroke on the whiteboard and have the student erase it with a smooth motion with her pointer finger.

Write swing three more times. As you write it say, "swing." ***swing***
Which swing is the best? ***answers vary***
Why? ***answers vary***

Point to the one you think is the best and explain why. Draw a silly smiley face next to the best one.

Writing on Paper

1.3 Handwriting Practice

Demonstrate to the student the correct way to hold a pencil. The student should grasp the pencil with the thumb and pointer finger while resting the pencil on the middle finger.

Write the swing stroke two times on each line of the worksheet.

Look at your swing strokes. Which one is the neatest?

Which line size feels the easiest to write on?

Teacher Tip

Some children are not ready for writing with a pencil and paper. The handwriting worksheets are optional for all students. Practice writing using large motor movements until the child has developed the needed fine motor skills. Encourage fine motor development by providing opportunities to bead, work with LEGO®s, etc.

Teacher Tip

Though allowing some flexibility with pencil grip styles is respectful of students' learning preferences, it is vital for students to develop a grip that allows for fluid range of fine-motor movements. If the grip does not allow for a range of motion, the student's handwriting will suffer. It is always easier to develop good habits from the beginning than to correct ingrained habits later.

LESSON 2

Objectives

HANDWRITING: Learn the down stroke. Review the lines and the swing stroke.

PHONEMIC AWARENESS: Develop a kinesthetic awareness of how sounds are formed. Practice blending two words into one word.

Materials

NEEDED: LOE whiteboard; blue, green, and red dry erase markers; Tactile Cards 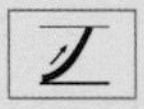 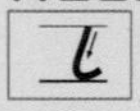 or 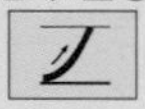 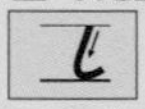 (swing, down).

OPTIONAL: Dr. Seuss book, LEGO®s, toy car

Phonemic Awareness

A Kinesthetic Awareness of Sounds

In the last lesson we began to learn about sounds. We learned that some sounds are voiced and some are unvoiced.

How can you tell if a sound is voiced or unvoiced? *Place your hand on your throat and see if it vibrates when you say the sound.*

Multi-Sensory Fun

If a student is struggling to feel the difference between voiced and unvoiced sounds, have her place her hand on your throat to feel the vibrations.

I will say a sound. Tell me if it is voiced or unvoiced. Place your hand on your throat to test each one.

/b/ *voiced*
/p/ *unvoiced*
/f/ *unvoiced*
/v/ *voiced*
/t/ *unvoiced*
/d/ *voiced*
/g/ *voiced*
/h/ *unvoiced*

Today we will do a new experiment with sounds.

Say the sound /m/. What is your mouth doing to say /m/? *My lips are closed.*
Is your voice box on or off when you say /m/? *on*
Where is the air coming out? *Answers will vary.*

Book List

Read a Dr. Seuss book each day this week. Encourage students to listen to how Dr. Seuss plays with sounds.

Put your hand in front of your nose and say /m/. Can you feel the air coming out your nose? ***yes***
Now try to say /m/ with your nose plugged. Can you do it? ***no***

/m/ is a called a nasal sound. Nasal is another word for nose.
If I have a nasal spray, what part of my body would it be for? ***your nose***
If I have nasal surgery, where did I have surgery? ***on your nose***
If I have a nasal voice **(speak in a nasal voice)**, where is most of the sound coming from? ***your nose***
Let's all speak in a nasal voice.

Say the sound /n/. What is your mouth doing when you say /n/. ***My tongue is on the top of my mouth. My lips are open a little bit.***
Is /n/ voiced or unvoiced? ***voiced***
Can you say /n/ with your nose plugged? ***no***
Is this a nasal sound? ***yes***
Why? ***The sound is coming from my nose.***

Now say /ng/. Where is your tongue? ***The middle of my tongue is pulled back and on the roof of my mouth.***
Is /ng/ voiced or unvoiced? ***voiced***
Say /n/ and /ng/. How are they different? ***With /n/ my tongue is near the front of my mouth. With /ng/ it is near the back of my mouth.***
Can you say /ng/ with your nose plugged? ***no***
What kind of sound is it? ***nasal***

Speech Tip

For students who struggle to articulate the /ng/ sound, direct them to first say /k/ and feel where the back of the tongue is touching the roof of the mouth in the back. Then direct the student to place his tongue up in that position, hold it, blow the air from his nose, and turn on his voicebox. For more tips see *Eliciting Sounds* pages 79-81.

Compound Words

2.1 Compound Words

LEGO®s

You have eight pictures on your page. I will say two words. Blend the words together. Shout out the answer and then circle the right picture.

snow man ***snowman***
row boat ***rowboat***
dog house ***doghouse***
tool box ***toolbox***
note book ***notebook***
cup cake ***cupcake***
high way ***highway***
tooth brush ***toothbrush***

Multi-Sensory Fun

Some students benefit by having an object to manipulate while blending. Say the first word and hold up one LEGO®. Say the second word and hold up the second LEGO®. Say each word closer together and hold the LEGO®s closer. Repeat. Finally snap the LEGO®s together and blend the word.

Handwriting

Reviewing the Lines

Take out your whiteboard.
Using your dry erase markers, put a blue dot on the baseline.
Put a green dot on the top line.
Put a red dot on the midline.

Repeat as needed.

Reviewing the Swing Stroke

Let's review the stroke we learned yesterday.

Show the Tactile Card or .

Demonstrate as you review the directions.

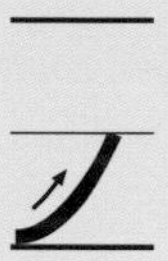

Start at the baseline. **Swing** up to the midline.

Start at the baseline. **Swing** up to the midline.

Now it is your turn to write the stroke with your pointer finger on the card (or on the whiteboard). ***swing***
Write the swing stroke in the air. ***swing***
Write the swing stroke with a marker on your whiteboard. ***swing***

The Down Stroke

Show the Tactile Card or .

Now we will learn the down stroke.

Demonstrate how to write the stroke using your pointer finger on the card while saying the directions aloud.

Start at the midline. **Down** to the baseline.

Notice the down stroke has a small hook on the end. This will connect into the next stroke of the letter or into the next word.

Start at the midline. **Down** to the baseline.

Notice the down stroke has a small hook on the end. This will connect into the next stroke of the letter.

Whiteboard
Blue, green, and red markers
Tactile Cards or
(swing, down)
Toy car

Teacher Tip

Each lesson will re-use Phonogram Cards and Tactile Cards from previous lessons. Keep all cards that have not been introduced bundled with a rubber band.Each day add the new cards to the stack of cards your students are learning.

Multi-Sensory Fun

Try writing the strokes by driving a toy car in the shape of the stroke.

Write the down stroke with your finger. Say, "down," as you write it. ***down***
Write the down stroke large in the air. ***down***
Pretend to write it on the desk with your pointer finger. ***down***
Pretend to write it on the door with your pointer finger. ***down***

Show the student the whiteboard.

Where does the down stroke start on the whiteboard?
at the midline

Point to the midline.

Write the down stroke with your pointer finger on the whiteboard. ***down***

Multi-Sensory Fun

Write the stroke on the whiteboard and have the student follow the motions to erase it with her pointer finger.

Now use a marker and write the down stroke on the whiteboard. ***down***

Write it three more times. As you write it say, "down." ***down***

Which down stroke is the best? ***Answers will vary.***
Why? ***Answers will vary.***

Point to the one you think is the best and explain why. Draw a star next to it.

Sometimes the down stroke starts on the top line. Watch me write it. Start at the top line, down all the way to the baseline, small hook.

You try it. ***Start at the top line, down.***

Now I will tell you where to start. Then write the down stroke.

top line	midline
midline	top line

Air Writing

I will call out a stroke. Write it big in the air with your pointer finger. As you write it, shout the name of the stroke.

down ***down***	swing ***swing***
swing ***swing***	down ***down***
down ***down***	down ***down***

Writing the Strokes

I will say a stroke. Write it on your whiteboard on the side with big lines. As you write the stroke, say the directions aloud.

swing ***swing***	down ***down***
down ***down***	swing ***swing***

Writing on Paper

2.2 Handwriting Practice

Write the down stroke two times on each line of the worksheet.

Look at your down strokes. Which one is the neatest?

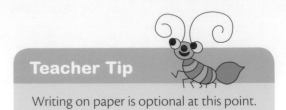

Teacher Tip

Writing on paper is optional at this point.

LESSON 3

Objectives

HANDWRITING: Learn the roll stroke.

PHONEMIC AWARENESS: Practice distinguishing sounds from one another. Learn to auditorily blend sounds into words.

Materials

NEEDED: LOE whiteboard, Tactile Card 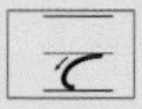 or 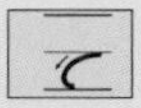 (roll)

OPTIONAL: Dr. Seuss book, a collection of toy animals, ball

Phonemic Awareness

Teacher Tip

Students with weak auditory processing skills often struggle with reading. These activities help students develop a kinesthetic awareness of sounds and provide additional tools for distinguishing sounds, which is necessary for becoming fluent readers and spellers.

Review

Say a sound. It can be a sound we talked about or one that you make up. It should only be one sound. Then tell me how you made it. *Answers will vary.*

What does it mean if a sound is voiced? *You turn on your voice box to say the sound.*

How can you test if a sound is voiced or unvoiced? *Place your hand on your throat and feel if it vibrates.*

I will say a sound. Repeat the sound, then tell me if it is voiced or unvoiced.

/g/	*/g/ voiced*	/d/	*/d/ voiced*
/h/	*/h/ unvoiced*	/m/	*/m/ voiced*
/t/	*/t/ unvoiced*	/b/	*/b/ voiced*
/sh/	*/sh/ unvoiced*	/p/	*/p/ unvoiced*

What is a nasal sound? *When the air comes out your nose. You cannot say it with your nose plugged.*

How can you test if a sound is a nasal sound? *Plug your nose and say the sound. If you can't say it with your nose plugged, it is a nasal sound.*

Now I will say a sound. Repeat the sound. Then tell me if it is a nasal sound or not.

/m/ ***/m/ nasal***
/sh/ ***/sh/ no***
/h/ ***/h/ no***
/n/ ***/n/ nasal***
/k/ ***/k/ no***
/b/ ***/b/ no***
/ng/ ***/ng/ nasal***
/t/ ***/t/ no***

Listening for Sounds in Isolation

Today we will practice listening for sounds.

The first sound is /m/. ***/m/***
When you hear me say /m/, jump up and rub your tummy as if you were saying, "/mmmm/, that tastes good."
If you do not hear /m/, sit quietly and listen closely.

What sound are you listening for? ***/m/***

/t/
/m/ ***/m/***
/l/
/m/ ***/m/***
/h/
/ng/
/m/ ***/m/***
/m/ ***/m/***

Multi-Sensory Fun

If a students struggles to identify if two sounds are the same, 1) draw attention to what your mouth looks like when you say the target sound, or 2) encourage the student to repeat the target sound followed by the sound that they misstated. Ask the student to feel if his mouth is in the same position for each sound.

Very good. Now listen for the sound /sh/. When you hear the sound /sh/, jump up, put your finger over your lips, and say /sh/.

What sound are you listening for? ***/sh/***

/s/
/t/
/sh/ ***/sh/***
/sh/ ***/sh/***
/b/
/j/
/r/
/sh/ ***/sh/***
/s/
/z/
/sh/ ***/sh/***

Book List

Read a Dr. Seuss book each day this week. Encourage students to listen to how Dr. Seuss plays with sounds.

Very good. Now listen for the sound /b/. When you hear the sound /b/, jump up and rock your arms as if you are holding a baby.

What sound are you listening for? ***/b/***

/b/ ***/b/***
/t/
/m/
/n/
/b/ ***/b/***
/p/
/b/ ***/b/***
/d/
/p/
/b/ ***/b/***

Blending Words Together

3.1 Blending Words Together

Words are made of sounds blended together. You have a page with pictures of animals. I will say the name of an animal with all the sounds "un-glued" or segmented. "Glue" or blend the sounds back together. When you know which animal it is, say it and point to the picture.

/c-ă-t/	*cat*
/p-ĭ-g/	*pig*
/d-ŏ-g/	*dog*
/b-er-d/	*bird*
/f-r-ŏ-g/	*frog*
/k-ow/	*cow*
/h-or-s/	*horse*
/m-ow-s/	*mouse*

Toy animals

Multi-Sensory Fun

Collect toy animals. Rather than using the pictures, show the children the animals. Segment the names for the animals and have the children blend them back together and select the correct animal.

Teacher Tip

If the student struggles to blend the sounds into a word, have her repeat each sound, then repeat them again faster and faster until hopefully she hears the word blended.

Handwriting

Review

Hold up a whiteboard.

I have forgotten something. Where is the top line? *The student points.*

Where is the base line? *The student points.*

Where is the midline? *The student points.*

Where does a swing stroke start? *on the baseline*

Show me how to write a swing stroke.

Start at the midline. Show me how to write a down stroke.

Start at the top line. Show me how to write a down stroke.

Whiteboard

Tactile Card or (roll)

Ball

Multi-Sensory Fun

For students who struggle to write the stroke on the whiteboard, ask them to write with their pointer finger on the Tactile Cards.

The Roll Stroke

Show the Tactile Card or .

Today we will learn a new stroke. This stroke is called the roll stroke.

Demonstrate the stroke on the Tactile Card as you explain the directions.

Multi-Sensory Fun

Before teaching the roll stroke, show the students a ball. Roll the ball from the student's right to the student's left. Have the student practice rolling the ball in the direction of the Roll Stroke (right to left).

Start at the midline. **Roll** around to the baseline.

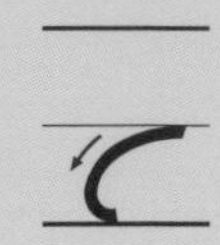

Start at the midline. **Roll** around to the baseline.

Write the roll stroke with your pointer finger. Say "roll" as you write it. ***roll***
Write the roll stroke two more times. ***roll, roll***

Show the student the whiteboard.

Where would you start to write the roll stroke on the whiteboard? ***at the midline***

Point to the midline.

Write the roll stroke with your pointer finger on the whiteboard two times. ***roll, roll***

Now use a marker and write the roll stroke on the whiteboard. ***roll***
Write it three more times. As you write it say "roll." ***roll***

Which roll stroke is the best? ***answers vary***
Why? ***answers vary***

Point to the one you think is the best and explain why. Draw a star next to the best one.

Simon Says

Let's play Simon Says. I will be Simon. When I say "Simon says," show me the stroke that I said. If I do not say "Simon says" first, then freeze.

Simon says, "roll."
Swing.
Simon says, "swing."
Simon says, "down."
Roll…

Teacher Tip

Some students struggle with writing in the air, others struggle with writing on the whiteboard. Allow students to choose if they want to write the stroke for Simon Says in the air, on the large lines of the whiteboard or on the small lines of the whiteboard.

Writing on Paper

3.2 Handwriting Practice

Write the roll stroke two times on each line of the worksheet using a pencil.
Look at your roll strokes. Which one is the neatest?
Write the down and swing strokes one time each on your favorite line size.

Teacher Tip

Remember, writing on paper is optional.

LESSON 4

Objectives

HANDWRITING: Learn the curve stroke or the straight stroke.

PHONEMIC AWARENESS: Listen for /th/ and /TH/. Practice blending words together.

Materials

NEEDED: LOE whiteboard; red, black, and blue dry erase markers; Tactile Card 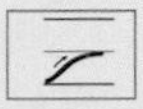 (curve) or 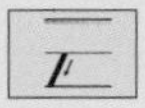 (straight)

OPTIONAL: Dr. Seuss book, dress-up clothes, blender, frozen fruit, juice, candy bar with segments, picture of an ant, shaving cream and tray

Phonemic Awareness

Listening for /th/ and /TH/

Today we will practice two new sounds. Let's begin with the sound /th/.

What does your mouth do when you say /th/? ***The tip of my tongue is between my teeth. Then I blow air out.***

Is your voice box on? ***no***

Can you say /th/ with your nose plugged? ***yes***

I am going to pretend to say a sound. Watch my mouth and tell me if I am saying /th/. If I say /th/, you say the sound /th/. If I say a different sound, shake your head "no."

Whisper the sounds quietly and encourage students to watch your mouth.

/b/
/th/ ***/th/***
/w/
/ē/
/th/ ***/th/***
/m/...

Teacher Tip

/th/ represents the unvoiced sound as found in *thin*, *think*, and *thought*.
/TH/ represents the voiced sound as found in *this*, *these*, and *that*.

Teacher Tip

Many young students do not pronounce the sounds /th/ and /TH/ correctly. This lesson will help them to become more aware of these sounds by feeling how to pronounce them, watching the teacher pronounce them, and listening for the sound.

Book List

Read a Dr. Seuss book each day this week. Encourage students to listen to how Dr. Seuss plays with sounds.

Our next sound is /TH/.
What is your mouth doing when you say /TH/? ***The tip of my tongue is between my teeth. Then I blow air.***
What is the difference between /th/ and /TH/. ***/th/ is unvoiced. /TH/ is voiced.***

Now I will say a sound. If I say /TH/, then you should say /TH/ as loudly as you can. If I say a different sound, be as quiet as a mouse.

/t/
/TH/ ***/TH/***
/TH/ ***/TH/***
/ng/
/sh/
/TH/ ***/TH/***
/h/
/s/...

Blending Words Together

4.1 Blending Words Together

What do you see on your page today? ***I see pictures of clothes: shorts, dress, hat, scarf, socks, shoes, boots, shirt.***

I will say a word so that all the sounds are segmented. Blend the sounds back together. When you know the word, say it and point to the picture.

/h-ă-t/ ***hat***
/b-oo-t-s/ ***boots***
/sh-or-t-s/ ***shorts***
/s-ŏ-k-s/ ***socks***
/d-r-ĕ-s/ ***dress***
/s-k-ar-f/ ***scarf***
/sh-oo-z/ ***shoes***
/sh-er-t/ ***shirt***

Speech Tip

If a student is struggling to say the sounds /th/ and /TH/, demonstrate how to form the sound. To say /th/, put the tip of your tongue between your teeth and blow. To say /TH/, put the tip of your tongue between your teeth, blow, and turn on your voice box.

Multi-Sensory Fun

If a student mishears a sound, encourage him to repeat the target sound followed by the sound that he misstated. Ask the student to feel if his mouth is in the same position for each sound.

Challenge

Direct the student to say sounds while you will listen for /th/ or /TH/. Repeat the sound when the student says /th/ or /TH/. Shake your head "no" when the student says a different sound.

Multi-Sensory Fun

Use real clothes for activity 4.1 Blending Words Together. Segment a word. The student should find the piece of clothing and put it on.

Vocabulary

Blend - Make a smoothie out of frozen fruit and juice using a blender. Demonstrate how the pieces are combined to form a blend.
Segmented - Bring a candy bar. Show students how to break it into segments. Look at an ant. Discuss how the body is segmented.

Handwriting

Review

Take out your whiteboard.

Put a blue dot on the baseline.
Put a black dot on the midline.
Put a red dot on the top line.

I will say a stroke. Write the stroke, then show it to me.

down
roll
swing
roll
down
roll
swing

Whiteboard
Blue, black, red markers
Tactile Card (curve for cursive)
or (straight for manuscript)
Shaving cream and tray

Multi-Sensory Fun

Practice writing the stokes in shaving cream.

The Curve Stroke & The Straight Stroke

Today we will learn the curve (straight) stroke.

Show the Tactile Card or .

Demonstrate the stroke as you explain the directions.

Teacher Tip

In this lesson there are different strokes for manuscript and cursive. The cursive directions are in the green box. The manuscript are in the blue box. In the dialog, manuscript directions are in parentheses.

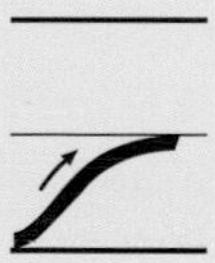

Start at the baseline. **Curve** up to the midline.

Start at the midline. **Straight** to the baseline.

Practicing writing the stroke using your pointer finger.

Show the student the whiteboard.

Where would you start to write the curve (straight) stroke on the whiteboard? ***at the baseline (midline)***

Point to the baseline (midline).

Write the curve (straight) stroke with your pointer finger on the whiteboard two times.

Now use a marker to write the curve (straight) stroke on the whiteboard.

Multi-Sensory Fun

Direct students to "write" the stroke with their pointer finger anyplace in the room. For example: on a table, the wall, a window, a chair, their leg...

Write it three more times.
Which one is the best? ***answers vary***
Why? ***answers vary***

Point to the one you think is the best and explain why. Draw a smiley face next to the best one.

Simon Says

Let's play Simon Says. I will be Simon. When I say "Simon says," write the stroke that I said in the air. If I do not say "Simon says" first, then freeze.

Simon says, "curve." (or "straight.")
Swing.
Simon says, "roll."
Simon says, "down."
Swing.
Simon says, "swing."...

Treasure Hunt

Tactile Cards

Hide the Tactile Cards that have been learned so far around the room. Ask the student to find the cards. When she finds one, she should bring it back, write the stroke on the card with her pointer finger, and say the name of the stroke.

Writing on Paper

4.2 Handwriting Practice

Write the curve (straight) stroke two times on each line of the worksheet.
Which one is the neatest?
Write the roll and down strokes one time each on your favorite line size.

LESSON 5

Objectives

HANDWRITING: Learn the phonogram a.

PHONEMIC AWARENESS: Compare the sounds /s/, /z/, and /th/. Distinguish sounds in isolation. Practice blending sounds into words.

Materials

NEEDED: LOE whiteboard, timer, a children's book, Phonogram Card a, Tactile Card a or a, *Doodling Dragons: An ABC Book of Sounds*

OPTIONAL: Dr. Seuss book, foods and activities for "a" Day

Phonemic Awareness

Comparing the Sounds /s/, /z/, and /th/

Timer

I will say a sound. Join me in saying it. */s-s-s-s/*

Hold the sound as the students join you in saying it.

How long can you say /s/?

Time the students.

Put your hand in front of your mouth. Say /s/ and feel the air coming out of your mouth.

I will say a new sound. Repeat the sound with me. */z-z-z-z-z/*

What is the same between /s/ and /z/? ***The mouth is in the same position.***
Why do they sound different? ***/s/ is unvoiced and /z/ is voiced.***
Can you change between /s/ and /z/ without letting the air stop? ***/s-s-z-z-s-z/***

Let's compare /s/ and /th/.
Say /s/. ***/s/***

Speech Tip

Many young students confuse the sounds /s/ and /th/. Help students to compare the sounds by showing them the shape of your mouth and position of your tongue for each sound. Notice the tongue sticks out slightly in front of the teeth to say /th/, whereas with the /s/ sound the tongue is pulled back inside the mouth behind the top teeth. Allow them to feel the stream of air that is present with both sounds. Explain how the air is flowing over the tongue for both sounds. The difference is the position of the tongue.

Now say /th/. ***/th/***

How are these sounds different? ***With /th/ my tongue is sticking out a bit between my teeth. With /s/ my tongue is inside my mouth.***

Book List

Read a Dr. Seuss book each day this week. Encourage students to listen to how Dr. Seuss plays with sounds.

Listening for Sounds in Isolation

Now we will listen for a sound. The first sound is /t/. When I say /t/, stand up.

What sound are we listening for? ***/t/***

/s/	/j/
/b/	/d/
/g/	/t/ ***student stands up***

When you hear me say /ng/, jump.

What sound are we listening for? ***/ng/***

/n/	/ĭ/
/m/	/t/
/ŏ/	/ng/ ***student jumps***

Now we will listen for /s/. When I say /s/, you should lie down.

What sound are we listening for? ***/s/***

/th/	/z/
/w/	/s/ ***student lays down***
/TH/	

When you hear me say /TH/, clap your hands.

What sound are we listening for? ***/TH/***

/p/	/ă/
/z/	/k/
/y/	/s/
/w/	/TH/ ***student claps***

Blending Words Together

I will segment a word. When you know the word, say it, and act it out.

/s-ĭ-t/	***sit***	/s-ĭ-ng/	***sing***
/h-ŏ-p/	***hop***	/s-p-ĭ-n/	***spin***
/s-t-ă-n-d/	***stand***	/d-ă-n-s/	***dance***
/l-ă-f/	***laugh***	/t-w-er-l/	***twirl***
/j-u-m-p/	***jump***	/s-m-ī-l/	***smile***
/w-ä-k/	***walk***	/k-r-ī/	***cry***
/r-ŭ-n/	***run***	/t-ă-p/	***tap***

The Phonogram a

The Phonogram a

To learn how to read a book, we need to begin by learning how to read the pictures for each sound. These pictures of sounds are called phonograms. A phonogram is a picture of a sound.

Phono means sound. Can you think of any other words that have "phone" in them? ***telephone, cell phone, megaphone*** A telephone and a cell phone are both ways to hear sounds. A megaphone makes sounds louder.

When people invented writing, they decided to make up symbols to represent the sounds.

Hold up a book and point to examples of phonograms, words, and sentences.

The phonograms or sounds combine together into words. The words combine together into sentences. And the sentences combine together into books and stories.

In order to learn to read, you need to learn all the pictures for the sounds in English.

Today we will learn our first phonogram. However, before we begin, I have a question. What are some of the sounds a dog makes? ***growl, bark, whine, howl***

In the same way that a dog makes more than one sound, some of our phonograms will make more than one sound.

Show the Phonogram Card a.

This phonogram says /ă-ā-ä/.
Say it with me. ***/ă-ā-ä/***
How many sounds is /ă-ā-ä/? ***three***
Let's march around the room saying /ă-ā-ä/. ***/ă-ā-ä/***

5.1 The Phonogram a

Some phonograms have more than one way they will appear in books. In your workbook is a page with some pictures of /ă-ā-ä/. What do you notice about them?

Let the child make observations.

Whiteboard
Phonogram Card a
A children's book
Food and activities for "a" Day

Multi-Sensory Fun

A fun way to increase phonemic awareness is to integrate activities, foods, and games that use the target phonogram.

a Day

Eat apples, adzuki beans, apricots, angel food cake, almonds, angel hair pasta, animal crackers, avocado, and asparagus. Find acorns. Learn about animals such as apes, ants, anteaters, alligators, and antelope. Read a book about acrobats. Watch a movie about astronauts.

Teacher Tip

Learning all the sounds for each phonogram right from the beginning helps to prevent confusion, teaches the students there is a pattern to the language, and eliminates unnecessary exceptions.

Teacher Tip

At this point you should always refer to phonograms by their sound(s). Do not introduce the letter names. In order to learn to read, students must master the sounds. Letter names are only useful for communicating spellings. Letter names will be introduced with the uppercase letters beginning in Level B.

Doodling Dragons: Sounds in Words

Open to the A page in *Doodling Dragons.*
Point to the phonogram [a] on the page.

What does this say? ***/ă-ā-ä/***
Listen as I read the poem.

Read the /ă-ā-ä/ page aloud.

Point to the phonogram [a] on the page.

How many sounds does this make? ***three***

Now I will read the poem again. If you hear /ă/ in a word, raise your hand.

Read the /ă-ā-ä/ page, exaggerating the /ă/ sound.

Now I will read it again. If you hear /ā/ in a word, shout out /ā/.

Read the /ă-ā-ä/ page aloud, exaggerating the /ā/ sound.

/ä/ sounds like a sleepy sound to me.
Say /ä/ while opening your mouth big and stretching.

Now I will read it again. If you hear /ä/ in a word, stretch and say /ä/.

Read the /ă-ā-ä/ page aloud, exaggerating the /ä/ sound.

Doodling Dragons

Teacher Tip

The purpose of this activity is to build awareness of the sounds in words. Do not expect kids to hear all the instances of the /ă-ā-ä/ phonogram in the words.

Challenge

Look at the "a" page. Segment a word from the picture aloud. For example /ă-n-t-s/. Ask the student to point to the correct picture.

Handwriting

Writing the Phonogram [a]

Now we will learn how to write /ă-ā-ä/.

5.1 The Phonogram a

Show Tactile Card [a] or [a]

This is how /ă-ā-ä/ looks when we write it. Look at the pictures of /ă-ā-ä/ in your workbook. Which one does it look the closest to?

Whiteboard
Phonogram Card [a]
Tactile Card [a] or [a]

Cursive Only: Show the Phonogram Card [a] and the Tactile Card [a].
Notice the stroke in front of /ă-ā-ä/. This stroke will help us to connect /ă-ā-ä/ to the other phonograms in a word. Then we will not need to lift up our pencils so much.

When we write phonograms, we will combine the strokes we have been learning. I will show you step by step how to write each phonogram. If you feel confused, let me know and I can show you again.

We will begin by writing each step of the phonogram with our pointer finger on the Tactile Card (or on the whiteboard).

Teacher Tip

Some students need the full directions for writing, while others prefer the shortened directions which are the same as the stroke names.

①**Curve** up to the midline, ②**roll** back around to the baseline, ③**swing** up to the midline, ④**down** to the baseline. /ă-ā-ä/

All the cursive letters begin on the baseline.

Demonstrate step 1.
Start at the baseline. Curve up to the midline.

Now it is your turn. Tell me the steps as you write it. *Curve up to the midline.*

Demonstrate steps 1 and 2.
Curve up to the midline, roll back around to the baseline. *Curve up to the midline, roll around to the baseline.*

Demonstrate steps 1, 2, and 3.
Curve up to the midline, roll back around to the baseline, swing up to the midline. *Curve up to the midline, roll around to the baseline, swing up to the midline.*

Demonstrate steps 1, 2, 3, and 4.
Curve up to the midline, roll back around to the baseline, swing up to the midline, down to the baseline. /ă-ā-ä/ *Curve up to the midline, roll around to the baseline, swing up to the midline, down to the baseline. /ă-ā-ä/*

Start at the midline. ①**Roll** around to the baseline, ②**swing** up to the midline, ③**straight** to the baseline. /ă-ā-ä/

Before writing a phonogram, it is important to know where it starts.

/ă-ā-ä/ begins on the midline.

Demonstrate step 1.
Start at the midline. Roll around to the baseline.

Now it is your turn. Tell me the steps as you write it. *Start at the midline. Roll around to the baseline.*

Demonstrate steps 1 and 2.
Start at the midline. Roll around to the baseline, swing up to the midline. *Start at the midline, roll around to the baseline, swing up to the midline.*

Demonstrate steps 1, 2, and 3.
Start at the midline. Roll around to the baseline, swing up to the midline, straight to the baseline. /ă-ā-ä/ *Start at the midline, roll around to the baseline, swing up to the midline, straight to the baseline. /ă-ā-ä/*

Practice writing /ă-ā-ä/ two times using your pointer finger on the Tactile Card (or on the whiteboard). As you do, tell me the directions aloud.

Each of our phonograms will also have short directions which help us to write the phonogram easily and with rhythm.

This is how we will write /ă-ā-ä/ from now on:

Demonstrate how to write the phonogram emphasizing the rhythm.

Curve, roll, swing, down. /ă-ā-ä/ Your turn. ***Curve, roll, swing, down. /ă-ā-ä/***	Start at the midline, roll, swing, straight. /ă-ā-ä/ Your turn. ***Start at the midline, roll, swing, straight. /ă-ā-ä/***

Write /ă-ā-ä/ three times with your pointer finger. As you write it, say the short directions.

Let's write /ă-ā-ä/ in the air with our arm.
Write /ă-ā-ä/ in the air with your pinkie finger.

Multi-Sensory Fun

If the student is reluctant to write with a marker, write /ă-ā-ä/ on the whiteboard and have the student follow the strokes to erase it with her pointer finger as she says the strokes aloud.

Show the student the whiteboard.

Where would you start to write /ă-ā-ä/ on the whiteboard? ***at the baseline (midline)***

Write /ă-ā-ä/ with your pointer finger on the whiteboard.

Now use a marker to write /ă-ā-ä/ on the whiteboard.
Write /ă-ā-ä/ three more times.
Which one is the best? ***answers vary***
Why? ***answers vary***

Point to the one you think is the best and explain why. Draw a star next to the best one.

Show the Phonogram Card a.

What does this say? ***/ă-ā-ä/***

Writing on Paper

5.2 Handwriting Practice

Write /ă-ā-ä/ three times on each line of the worksheet.
Which one is the neatest?
On which line is it easiest to write /ă-ā-ä/?

REVIEW LESSON A

Area	Skill	Mastery
Phonemic Awareness	Recognize voiced and unvoiced sounds.	3
	Blend two words into a compound word.	1
	Blend one-syllable CVC words.	2
	Listen for sounds in isolation.	3
Handwriting	Identify lines and their names.	1
	Write the swing, down, and roll stroke.	2
	Write the curve stroke - cursive.	2
	Write the straight stroke - manuscript.	2
	Write the phonogram a.	3
Phonograms	Read the phonogram a.	2

About Assessments

For the Teacher

Following every fifth lesson there will be a review lesson. This lesson will provide teachers with an opportunity to assess the student and provide additional practice. Teachers will also gain a better understanding of what material should be mastered, and what content the student must only be familiar with in order to move on to the next lessons.

Young students should not be given grades, or passed on without these foundational skills.

Rather, all students should be taught to the point of mastery. Assessments should inform the teacher which skills need additional practice or which students may require additional help.

Each skill area is included on the chart. Skills with a 1 should be mastered before students move on to the next lesson. Skills with a 2 should be familiar to the child, but the child can still be working towards mastery. For skills marked with a 2, students should demonstrate familiarity but not necessarily answer all the questions correctly. These skills will be practiced extensively in the upcoming lessons. Skills with a 3 do not need to be mastered in order for students to move on. Some activities labeled with a 3 will be covered extensively in later lessons. Other level 3 skills are not necessary for becoming strong readers and spellers, but they have proved beneficial for some students. Level 3 skills are listed in the chart, but they are not included in the assessments.

Remember, all students and classes are different. Curriculum provides a structure and ideas for teaching, but ultimately it is up to the teacher to exercise the art of teaching and to determine the pace and amount of review needed for your students. Students who master these foundational skills early will save countless hours later in remediation, as well as frustration. Therefore, use the information from the assessments to review as needed before advancing to the next lessons.

Phonemic Awareness Assessment

Blending Compound Words

Ball

Basket or box

Teacher Tip

Ask each student 1-3 words. Use the additional words for practice if needed.

Set up a basket in the room.

If in a classroom, seat the children in a circle around the basket.

I will pass you the ball. Then I will say two words. "Glue" or blend the words together into a new word. When you know the word, say it aloud. Then you may try to make a basket with the ball.

clothes line	*clothesline*	grand pa	*grandpa*
sun flower	*sunflower*	grass hopper	*grasshopper*
rail road	*railroad*	thunder storm	*thunderstorm*
grand mother	*grandmother*	key board	*keyboard*
tooth pick	*toothpick*	bed room	*bedroom*
book shelf	*bookshelf*	river bank	*riverbank*
air plane	*airplane*	week end	*weekend*
eye ball	*eyeball*	bath tub	*bathtub*
air port	*airport*	water fall	*waterfall*

book mark *bookmark*
sun set *sunset*
rain bow *rainbow*
grand ma *grandma*
foot ball *football*
kick stand *kickstand*
class room *classroom*

Blending One-Syllable Words

A.1 One-Syllable Words

On your page you have eight pictures. I will segment two of the words. Circle the correct picture.

/b-ĕ-d/ *bed*
/m-oo-n/ *moon*

Teacher Tip

At this stage students should begin to blend one-syllable CVC (Consonant-Vowel-Consonant) words. Many students will still struggle with words that begin or end with a consonant blend.

Handwriting Assessment

Handwriting

A.2 Handwriting

Students should be able to form the stroke using large motor motions on the handwriting chart or whiteboard. They do not need to be able to write the stroke with pencil and paper to move on to the next lesson.

Choose whether to have the students use the Handwriting Chart A.2 or use whiteboards.

Repeat questions as needed. Show students how to write the stroke if it was forgotten. This is acceptable for mastery at this stage.

You have eight blocks in front of you. Today I will ask you to write something. If you write it correctly, you can put one block in place on your tower.

Put a blue dot on the top line.
Put a black dot on the midline.
Put a red dot on the baseline.
Write a swing stroke.
Write a down stroke.
Write a roll stroke.
Write a curve (straight) stroke.
Write /ă-ā-ä/.

Whiteboard
Blue, black, and red markers
Eight LEGO®s or blocks per student

Multi-Sensory Fun

Provide the student with eight blocks or LEGO®s. Each time she writes correctly, she may put a block on the tower. At the end, she may knock down the tower.

Teacher Tip

Teachers should set the standards for individual students for handwriting. Some students struggle with handwriting due to their age or learning strengths and weaknesses. There is no reason to hold the child back from learning to read because of handwriting. Continue to practice writing with short, respectful games and activities, and allow the student to keep progressing in the lessons.

Optional Practice Ideas

Blending Compound Words

Play games using the words found on the following pages.
"1.1 Compound Words" on page 2
"2.1 Compound Words" on page 7
"Blending Compound Words" on page 26

If the student is particularly struggling with this concept, try the idea found in "Multi-Sensory Fun" on page 7.

Blending One-Syllable Words

Many students struggle with blending, especially if the word includes a consonant blend. If the student blended one or two words correctly, go ahead and move on to the next lesson. This concept will be practiced extensively in later lessons.

If you desire to practice further before moving ahead, play "Dress-Up Blending" by putting out a pile of dress-up clothes. Segment a word and ask the student to pick out the piece of clothing and put it on.

Or segment active words with an activity such as "Blending Words Together" on page 20.

Handwriting Practice

Practice writing the strokes in the air by playing Simon Says, or write them in sensory materials such as sand, salt, or shaving cream.

LESSON 6

Objectives

HANDWRITING: Learn the phonogram d.

PHONEMIC AWARENESS: Distinguish sounds in isolation. Practice blending sounds into words.

Materials

NEEDED: LOE whiteboard, crayons, Phonogram Cards a and d, *Doodling Dragons*, Tactile Card d or d, sensory box

OPTIONAL: Foods and activities for "d" Day

Phonemic Awareness

Blending Active Words

I will say a word. When you know the word, shout it and act it out.

/j-ŭ-m-p/	*jump*
/s-p-ĭ-n/	*spin*
/s-ĭ-t/	*sit*
/l-ă-f/	*laugh*
/k-r-ī/	*cry*
/sh-ow-t/	*shout*
/t-ä-k/	*talk*
/wh-ĭ-s-p-er/	*whisper*
/h-ŏ-p/	*hop*
/r-ŭ-n/	*run*
/s-ĭ-ng/	*sing*
/d-ă-n-s/	*dance*
/t-w-er-l/	*twirl*
/f-r-ē-z/	*freeze*
/k-l-ă-p/	*clap*
/f-ä-l/	*fall*
/k-r-ä-l/	*crawl*
/r-ō-l/	*roll*

Vocabulary

Discuss the differences in meaning between laugh, cry, shout, talk, and whisper.

6.1 One-Syllable Words

Crayons

On your page you have some pictures. I will segment a word. Say the word and color the picture.

/k-ă-t/ *cat*
/d-ŏ-g/ *dog*
/h-or-s/ *horse*
/p-ĭ-g/ *pig*
/sh-ē-p/ *sheep*
/b-er-d/ *bird*
/f-ĭ-sh/ *fish*
/s-n-ā-k/ *snake*

Listening for Sounds

We have been exploring sounds and learning how our mouth, tongue, and voice box work together to make the sounds that we speak.

Close your eyes. I will say a sound. Say it back to me. If I say the sound softly, say it back softly. If I say it loudly, say it loudly. If I say it in a silly voice, use a silly voice.

Speech Tip

Some students may be missing the /l/ sound in their speech. Tell the student to say /n/. Then relax the tongue slightly and blow air over the top of the tongue.

/m/ ***/m/***
/t/ ***/t/***
/g/ ***/g/***
/s/ ***/s/***
/oy/ ***/oy/***
/ŏ/ ***/ŏ/***
/l/ ***/l/***
/sh/ ***/sh/***
/TH/ ***/TH/***
/oo/ ***/oo/***
/k/ ***/k/***
/th/ ***/th/***
/p/ ***/p/***

Very good! Open your eyes.
Now we will listen for a sound. The first sound is /oo/. When I say /oo/, spin in a circle.
What sound are we listening for? ***/oo/***

/sh/
/l/
/th/
/TH/
/oo/

When you hear /r/, march in place.
What sound are we listening for? ***/r/***

/ng/
/oy/
/t/
/d/
/w/
/s/
/m/
/r/

Speech Tip

If students struggle to hear the difference between /s/, /z/, /th/, and /TH/, encourage them to watch the speaker's lips, tongue, and teeth. Can they see a difference? Also practice listening for the difference between the voiced and unvoiced sounds.

Now we will listen for /z/. When you hear the sound /z/, pretend you are asleep and snoring.
What sound are we listening for? ***/z/***

/s/
/sh/
/v/
/x/
/TH/
/z/

Now we will listen for /TH/. When you hear the sound /TH/, pretend you are a car zooming around. What sound are we listening for? */TH/*

/th/	/s/
/w/	/z/
/m/	/TH/

The Phonogram d

The Phonogram d

Show the Phonogram Card a.

What does this say? */ă-ā-ä/*.

Show the Phonogram Card d.

This is our new phonogram. It says /d/.
What does it say? */d/*

Show the Phonogram Card a.
What does this say? */ă-ā-ä/*

Show the Phonogram Card d.
What does this say? */d/*

Now I will show them to you very fast. See if I can trick you.

Show the Phonogram Cards and have the students read them quickly.

Doodling Dragons: Sounds in Words

Today we will read the /d/ page in *Doodling Dragons*.

Point to the phonogram d on the page.
What does this say? */d/*
Listen as I read.

Read the /d/ page aloud.

Now I will read the poem again. If you hear /d/ in the words, raise your hand.

Read the /d/ page again emphasizing the /d/ sound.

Phonogram Card d

d Day

Eat dates, dark chocolate, dill pickles, Dove Bars, dumplings, and dried fruit for dinner. Go to a deli for lunch. Play a game in the dark. Pick dandelions and daisies. Read about deer, dogs, dinosaurs, dolphins, donkeys, doves, and ducks. Learn about dimes. Play with dump trucks and dolls. Read a story about a dragon.

Teacher Tip

Use every opportunity to refer to a phonogram by its sounds. At this stage do not introduce the letter names.

Doodling Dragons

Multi-Sensory Fun

Ask students to find "d" in their environment on packages, signs, books…

Challenge

Look at the "d" page. Segment a word from the picture aloud. Ask the student to point to the correct picture.

Handwriting

Review

Write /ă-ā-ä/ on the whiteboard. While you write it, tell me the directions.

Whiteboard
Phonogram Card d
Tactile Card d or d

Curve, roll, swing, down. /ă-ā-ä/

Start at the midline, roll, swing, straight. /ă-ā-ä/

Writing the Phonogram d

Let's learn how to write the sound /d/.

Show the Tactile Card d or d.

Teacher Tip

Some students find it easier to learn handwriting by beginning with the shortened directions. Experiment with your students to find out how they learn best.

Cursive Only: Show the Phonogram Card d and the Tactile Card d.

What do you notice is different between the phonogram card and how we write /d/? *There is a curve stroke in front of the /d/.*

This stroke will help us to connect /d/ to other phonograms in a word.

Demonstrate how to write /d/ using your pointer finger on the Tactile Card.

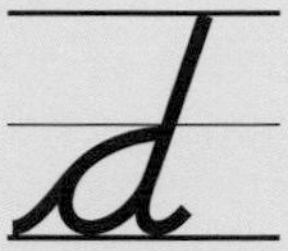

①**Curve** up to the midline, ②**roll** back around to the baseline, ③**swing tall** up to the top line, ④**down** to the baseline. /d/

Lowercase cursive letters all start at the baseline.

Curve up to the midline. Now it is your turn. Tell me the steps as you write it. ***Curve up to the midline.***

Curve up to the midline, roll back around to the baseline. ***Curve up to the midline, roll around to the baseline.***

Curve up to the midline, roll back around to the baseline, swing tall up to the top line. ***Curve up to the midline, roll around to the baseline, swing tall up to the top line.***

Curve up to the midline, roll back around to the baseline, swing tall up to the top line, down to the baseline. /d/ ***Curve up to the midline, roll around to the baseline, swing tall up to the top line, down to the baseline. /d/***

Start at the midline. ①**Roll** around to the baseline, ②**swing tall** up to the top line, ③**straight** to the baseline. /d/

Before writing a phonogram, it is important to know where it starts.

/d/ begins on the midline.

Start at the midline, roll around to the baseline. Now it is your turn. Tell me the steps as you write it. ***Start at the midline, roll around to the baseline.***

Start at the midline, roll around to the baseline, swing tall up to the top line. ***Start at the midline, roll around to the baseline, swing tall up to the top line.***

Start at the midline, roll around to the baseline, swing tall up to the top line, straight to the baseline. /d/ ***Start at the midline, roll around to the baseline, swing tall up to the top line, straight to the baseline. /d/***

The shortened directions for writing /d/ are like this:

Demonstrate how to write the phonogram, emphasizing the rhythm:

Curve, roll, swing tall, down. /d/ Your turn. ***Curve, roll, swing tall, down. /d/***

Start at the midline, roll, swing tall, straight. /d/ Your turn. ***Start at the midline, roll, swing tall, straight. /d/***

Write /d/ two times using your pointer finger. Be sure to say the shortened directions aloud.

With your arm, write /d/ in the air.
With your finger, write /d/ on the ground.
With your finger, write /d/ on the window.

Show the student the whiteboard.

Where would you start to write /d/ on the whiteboard? ***at the baseline (midline)***

Using your whiteboard, write the phonogram /d/ two times with your pointer finger.

Now use a marker to write /d/ on the whiteboard.
Write /d/ three more times.
Which one is the best? ***answers vary***
Why? ***answers vary***

Multi-Sensory Fun

For reluctant writers, write the phonogram on the whiteboard and direct the student to erase it with her finger or have the student write it on the Tactile Card with her pointer finger.

Point to the one you think is the best and explain why. Draw a star next to the best one.

Show the Phonogram Card d.

What does this say? ***/d/***

Sensory Writing

Sensory box with salt or cornmeal
Phonogram Cards a and d

Show the students a Phonogram Card. Have the students read the sound(s) then write the phonogram in the sensory box.

Writing on Paper

6.2 Handwriting Practice

Write /d/ three times on your favorite line size.
Which /d/ is the neatest?

LESSON 7

Objectives

HANDWRITING: Learn the drop-swoop stroke.

PHONEMIC AWARENESS: Listen for sounds at the beginning of words. Practice blending sounds into words.

Materials

NEEDED: Two LOE whiteboards, crayons or markers, Phonogram Cards a and d, Tactile Card or (drop-swoop), crackers or pennies to keep score, timer

OPTIONAL: Stickers

Phonemic Awareness

Vocabulary

Discuss the differences in meaning between stomp, walk, march, gallop, and prance.

Blending Active Words

I will say a word. When you know the word, say it and act it out.

/sh-ow-t/	*shout*
/wh-ĭ-s-p-er/	*whisper*
/w-ĭ-g-l/	*wiggle*
/f-r-ē-z/	*freeze*
/k-l-ă-p/	*clap*
/s-t-ŏ-m-p/	*stomp*
/w-ä-k/	*walk*
/m-ar-ch/	*march*
/g-ă-l-ŏ-p/	*gallop*
/p-r-ă-n-s/	*prance*
/d-ă-n-s/	*dance*
/s-ĭ-ng/	*sing*
/y-ĕ-l/	*yell*

Beginning Sounds

7.1 Beginning Sounds

You have a worksheet with pictures on it. Today we will listen for words that begin with a particular sound. I will say a sound. Repeat the sound, then look at the pictures and choose the picture that begins with the same sound. Then circle the picture.

/r/	*/r/ ring*	/s/	*/s/ sink*
/f/	*/f/ fire*	/b/	*/b/ ball*
/k/	*/k/ kite*	/d/	*/d/ duck*
/t/	*/t/ tent*		
/ă/	*/ă/ apple*		

Stickers

Multi-Sensory Fun

Provide the student with stickers. Ask her to cover the picture that starts with the same sound with a sticker.

Phonogram Practice

Review a and d

Show the Phonogram Card a.

What does this say? */ă-ā-ä/*

Show the Phonogram Card d.

What does this say? */d/*

I will show them to you quickly. Read the sound(s). How fast can you read them?

Alternate showing the Phonogram Cards d and a.

Phonogram Cards a and d

Handwriting

The Drop-Swoop Stroke

Whiteboard
Tactile Card 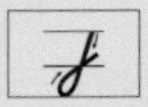 or 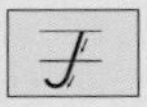
(drop-swoop stroke)

Today we will learn the drop-swoop stroke.

Demonstrate the stroke as you explain the directions.

Start at the midline. ①**Drop** down halfway below the baseline, ②**swoop**.

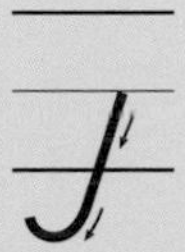

Start at the midline. ①**Drop** down halfway below the baseline, ②small **swoop**.

Practice writing the drop-swoop stroke with your pointer finger three times on the Tactile Card.

Write the drop-swoop stroke three times with a marker on your whiteboard.

Write It!

Whiteboard
Oyster crackers, M&M's, pennies, or other small treats to keep score

We will play a game to practice the strokes and phonograms we have learned.

Before we begin, remind me where each stroke and phonogram begins.

Point to where the down stroke begins. ***midline***

Where does the curve (straight) stroke begin? ***baseline (midline)***

Where does the roll stroke begin? ***midline***

Where does the drop-swoop stroke begin? ***midline***

Where does /ă-ā-ä/ begin? ***baseline (midline)***

Where does /d/ begin? ***baseline (midline)***

Teacher Tip

The stroke names in parentheses refer to manuscript handwriting.

Multi-Sensory Fun

Use large arm motions rather than a whiteboard.

I will call out a phonogram or the name of a stroke. Repeat it, write it, then show it to me. Each time you get one right, I will give you a (cracker). When you have ten (crackers), you "win" and you are finished. You may then enjoy the treat.

/ă-ā-ä/
drop-swoop
/d/
curve (or straight)
roll
down
swing...

Writing Race

Place two whiteboards on the opposite sides of the room from one another.

2 Whiteboards
Timer

When I call out a phonogram or handwriting stroke, you will run to the whiteboard, write the stroke, and show it to me.
Then I will call out another. You will then run to the other side of the room, write it, show it to me…

I will set the timer for one minute. How many phonograms and strokes do you think you can write in one minute?

/ă-ā-ä/
/d/
swing
down
roll
curve (or straight)
drop-swoop...

Classroom: Writing Relay

Divide the classroom into relay teams. Set up two whiteboards for each team. The first student in line runs, writes the stroke or phonogram, runs to the second whiteboard, writes it again, then runs back to tag the next person in line.

Writing on Paper

7.2 Handwriting Practice

Write the drop-swoop stroke three times on your favorite line size.

Write /ă-ā-ä/ and /d/ two (or three) times on your favorite line size.

LESSON 8

Objectives

HANDWRITING: Learn the phonogram g.

PHONEMIC AWARENESS: Listen for sounds at the beginning of words. Practice blending sounds into words.

Materials

NEEDED: LOE whiteboard, Phonogram Cards a, d, g, *Doodling Dragons*, Tactile Card g or g, sensory box

OPTIONAL: Foods and activities for "g" Day, sidewalk chalk or sheets of paper

Phonemic Awareness

Blending Treasure Hunt

I will say a word, segmented into sounds. When you know the word, run, find one in the room, and show it to me.

/p-ĕ-n/	*pen*
/b-ü-k/	*book*
/k-ō-t/	*coat*
/sh-oo-z/	*shoes*
/h-ă-t/	*hat*
/p-ĕ-n-s-ĭ-l/	*pencil*
/ē-r-ā-s-er/	*eraser*
/m-är-k-er/	*marker*
/k-ŭ-p/	*cup*
/p-ā-p-er/	*paper*
/s-p-oo-n/	*spoon*
/t-ā-b-l/	*table*

Beginning Sounds

8.1 Beginning Sounds

You have a worksheet with pictures on it. Today we are going to listen for words that begin with a particular sound. I will say a sound. Repeat the sound, then look at the pictures and choose the picture that begins with the same sound. Say the word, then circle the picture.

/s/	*/s/ sun*
/z/	*/z/ zebra*
/d/	*/d/ dog*
/k/	*/k/ cake*
/ch/	*/ch/ chicken*
/b/	*/b/ book*
/h/	*/h/ hand*
/sh/	*/sh/ sheep*

The Phonogram g

The Phonogram g

Show the Phonogram Card g.

This says /g-j/.

What does it say? ***/g-j/***

How many sounds is /g-j/? ***two***

March around the room saying /g-j/. ***/g-j/***

Phonogram Card g

g Day

Eat grapes, gingerbread, granola, green beans, gummy worms, and grapefruit. Make gingerbread men. Wear green and gold. Play games. Learn about geckos, gazelles, goats, geese, guppies, giraffes, gorillas, grasshoppers, grizzly bears, or goldfish. Make a gift for grandparents. Go to a jewelry store and look at gems.

8.2 The Phonogram g

Just like /ă-ā-ä/, /g-j/ has different shapes depending on the font used in the book. What is the same and what is different between these /g-j/'s?

Let the child make observations.

Doodling Dragons: Sounds in Words

Today we will read the /g-j/ page in *Doodling Dragons*.

Point to the phonogram g on the page.

What does this say? ***/g-j/***

Read the /g-j/ page aloud.

I will read it again. If you hear /g/ in the words, whisper, "g."

Read the page aloud, exaggerating the sound /g/.

Now if you hear /j/ in the words, jump up and down and shout, "j."

Read the page aloud, exaggerating the sound /j/.

Doodling Dragons

Challenge

Point to the giant. What sound of /g-j/ do you hear at the beginning of giant? /j/ What sound do you hear at the beginning of green? /g/...

Phonogram Hop

Lay the Phonogram Cards on the floor, or draw the phonograms outside on the sidewalk with sidewalk chalk.

I will call out a phonogram sound. When I do, jump on the phonogram you hear and say the sound(s).

/ă-ā-ä/

/g-j/

/d/...

Phonogram Cards a, d, g

Sidewalk chalk or sheets of paper

Classroom: Phonogram Hop

Write the phonograms on sheets of paper to lay on the floor. Have students work in pairs. One student reads the sound(s) while the other jumps.

Handwriting

Writing The Phonogram g

Whiteboard
Phonogram Card g
Tactile Card g or g

8.2 The Phonogram g

Show Tactile Card g or g

This is how /g-j/ looks when we write it. Look at the pictures of /g-j/ in your workbook. Which one does it look the closest to?

Cursive Only: Show the Phonogram Card g and the Tactile Card g.

What is different between the way that /g-j/ appears on the card and the way that we write it? *There is a curve stroke in front of /g-j/. The swoop comes up to the baseline.*

The swoop that comes up to the baseline will help us to connect to the next phonogram in the word.

Let's learn how to write the sound /g-j/.

Demonstrate how to write /g-j/ using the Tactile Card g or g.

①**Curve** up to the midline, ②**roll** back around to the baseline, ③**swing** up to the midline, ④**drop** down halfway below the baseline, ⑤**swoop.** /g-j/

Curve up to the midline.

Now it is your turn. Tell me the steps as you write it. ***Curve up to the midline.***

Curve up to the midline, roll back around to the baseline. ***Curve up to the midline, roll around to the baseline.***

Curve up to the midline, roll back around to the baseline, swing up to the midline. ***Curve up to the midline, roll around to the baseline, swing up to the midline.***

Curve up to the midline, roll back around to the baseline, swing up to the midline, drop down halfway below the baseline, swoop. /g-j/ ***Curve up to the midline, roll around to the baseline, swing up to the midline, drop down halfway below the baseline, swoop. /g-j/***

Start at the midline. ①**Roll** around to the baseline, ②**swing** up to the midline, ③**drop** down half-way below the baseline, ④small **swoop**. /g-j/

/g/ begins on the midline.

Start at the midline, roll around to the baseline. Now it is your turn. Tell me the steps as you write it. ***Start at the midline, roll around to the baseline.***

Start at the midline, roll around to the baseline, swing up to the midline. ***Start at the midline, roll around to the baseline, swing up to the midline.***

Start at the midline, roll around to the baseline, swing up to the midline, drop down halfway below the baseline, small swoop. /g-j/ ***Start at the midline, roll around to the baseline, swing up to the midline, drop down halfway below the baseline, small swoop. /g-j/***

The shortened directions for writing /g-j/ are like this:

Demonstrate how to write the phonogram, emphasizing the rhythm.

Curve, roll, swing, drop-swoop. /g-j/ ***Curve, roll, swing, drop-swoop. /g-j/***

Start at the midline, roll, swing, drop-swoop. /g-j/ ***Start at the midline, roll, swing, drop-swoop. /g-j/***

Write /g-j/ two times with your pointer finger. As you write it, say the short directions.

Let's write /g-j/ in the air with our arm.

Show the student the whiteboard.

Where would you start to write /g-j/ on the whiteboard? *at the baseline (midline)*

Write /g-j/ with your pointer finger on the whiteboard two times.

Now use a marker to write /g-j/ on the whiteboard.
Write /g-j/ three more times.
Which one is the best? *answers vary*
Why? *answers vary*

Point to the one you think is the best and explain why. Draw a star next to the best one.

Show the Phonogram Card g.

What does this say? */g-j/*

Matching Bookface and Written Phonograms

8.3 Matching Phonograms

Draw a line to match the bookface phonogram to the handwritten phonogram.

Sensory Writing

Sensory box with cornmeal or sand
Phonogram Cards a, d, g

Show the students a Phonogram Card. Have the student read the sound(s) then write the phonogram in the sensory box.

Writing on Paper

8.4 Handwriting Practice

Write /g-j/ three times on your favorite line size.
Which /g-j/ is the neatest?

LESSON 9

Objectives

HANDWRITING: Learn the phonogram c.

PHONEMIC AWARENESS: Listen for sounds at the beginning of words. Practice blending sounds into words.

Materials

NEEDED: LOE whiteboard, Phonogram Cards learned so far and c, Tactile Card c or c, *Doodling Dragons*, sidewalk chalk, beanbag, paper plates, markers or crayons

OPTIONAL: Foods and activities for "c" Day, stamp and ink

Phonemic Awareness

Beginning Sounds

9.1 Beginning Sounds

You have a worksheet with pictures on it. Today we will listen for words that begin with a particular sound. I will say a sound. Repeat the sound, then look at the pictures and choose the picture that begins with the same sound. Say the word, then circle the picture.

/ch/	*/ch/ chair*
/d/	*/d/ desk*
/s/	*/s/ saw*
/m/	*/m/ mop*
/l/	*/l/ lock*
/k/	*/k/ key*
/t/	*/t/ tree*
/f/	*/f/ fan*

Stamp
Ink

Multi-Sensory Fun

Provide the student with a stamp and ink pad. Have her stamp the picture that starts with the same sound.

Challenge

Inform students that you will say a sound. You want them to find something in the room that begins with the same sound. For example, /d/ door, desk, dots...

Blending Treasure Hunt

I will segment a word. When you know the word, run, find one in the room, and show it to me.

/p-ĕ-n-s-ĭ-l/	*pencil*
/t-oi/	*toy*
/p-ā-p-er/	*paper*
/k-ō-t/	*coat*
/d-ō-r/	*door*
/d-ŏ-l/	*doll*
/t-ā-b-l/	*table*
/r-ŭ-g/	*rug*
/ch-ā-r/	*chair*
/s-ĭ-n-k/	*sink*
/wh-ī-t-b-or-d/	*whiteboard*

Challenge

Ask the student to segment words and you find the object. Or in a classroom, chose a student to segment the words for the class.

Teacher Tip

Multi-syllable words are much more difficult to blend than one-syllable words. Mix in easy and difficult words as you play the game.

The Phonogram c

The Phonogram c

Using the Phonogram Cards, practice reading all the phonograms learned until this point.

Today we will learn a new phonogram.

Show the Phonogram Card c.

This says /k-s/. What does it say? */k-s/*

How many sounds is /k-s/? *two*

Let's read all the phonograms we have learned so far.

Phonogram Card c

c Day

Eat cake, carrots, ice cream cones, corn, and cabbage. Have kids color, pretend to go camping, play with cars, make cars and castles, and learn about cats and camels. Count pennies and talk about cents, cut out circles, and go cycling.

Doodling Dragons: Sounds in Words

Today we will read the /k-s/ page in *Doodling Dragons*.

Point to the phonogram c on the page.

What does this say? */k-s/*

Read the page two times. Ask students to listen for the sounds while you read the words.

Doodling Dragons

Challenge

Look at the "c" page. Segment a word from the picture aloud. Ask the student to point to the correct picture.

Handwriting

Writing the Phonogram c

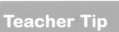

Let's learn how to write /k-s/.

Demonstrate how to write /k-s/ using Tactile Card c or c.

Whiteboard
Phonogram Card c
Tactile Card c or c

Cursive Only: Show the Phonogram Card c and the Tactile Card c.

What is the same and what is different between this /k-s/ and this /k-s/? *There is a curve stroke at the beginning of the cursive /k-s/.*

Teacher Tip

Some students find it easier to learn handwriting by beginning with the shortened directions. Experiment with your students to find out how they learn best.

①**Curve** around to just below the midline, ②**roll** back around to just above the baseline. /k-s/

Start just below the midline. ①**Roll** around to just above the baseline. /k-s/

Write /k-s/ two times with your pointer finger.
Using a marker, write /k-s/ on your whiteboard four times.

Which one is the best? *answers vary*

Point to the one you think is the best and explain why. Draw a heart next it.

Teacher Tip

From this point forward, handwriting instructions will not be repeated step by step in the Teacher's Manual. Teachers should continue to break down each step for their students. See page 42 to review how to dictate the steps.

Matching Phonograms

9.2 Matching Phonograms

Match the bookface and handwritten phonograms.

Phonogram Practice

Phonogram Aerobics

Today we will practice our phonograms by writing them in the air. I will say a sound(s). Write it as large as you can in the air. As you write it, say the strokes.

Multi-Sensory Fun

Call out a different body part to use to write the phonogram: pinkie finger, foot, elbow, nose.

/ă-ā-ä/

Curve, roll, swing, down. /ă-ā-ä/	*Start at the midline, roll, swing, straight. /ă-ā-ä/*

/k-s/

Curve, roll. /k-s/	*Start just below the midline, roll. /k-s/*

/d/

Curve, roll, swing tall, down. /d/	*Start at the midline, roll, swing tall, straight. /d/*

/g-j/

Curve, roll, swing, drop-swoop. /g-j/	*Start at the midline, roll, swing, drop-swoop. /g-j/*

Phonogram Hopscotch

Phonogram Cards
Sidewalk chalk
Beanbag

1) Draw a hopscotch board without anything in the squares. 2) Show the student a Phonogram Card. 3) Have him read it, then write it in the square of his choice. Fill in all the squares in this manner. 4) Direct the student to toss a beanbag onto one of the squares. 5) He then hops to the beanbag, reading each phonogram he passes, picks up the beanbag, and hops back again reading each of the sounds.

Indoor Phonogram Hopscotch

Phonogram Cards
Paper plates
Crayons or markers
Beanbag

Provide the student with four paper plates. Show the student a Phonogram Card. Have him read it, then write the phonogram on the plate. Continue until all four phonograms have been used. Use the paper plates to play Phonogram Hopscotch or Phonogram Relay.

Classroom: Phonogram Relay

One set of paper plate phonograms per team

1) Divide students into teams of 2-4 students. 2) Each team should set out one set of Phonogram Plates on the floor. 3) Each team then lines up behind their plates. 4) When the teacher says, "go," the first student should hop onto each plate and read the sound(s). 5) When he reaches the end, he turns around, runs back, and tags the next person in line.

Writing on Paper

9.3 Handwriting Practice

Write /k-s/ three times on your favorite line size.
Which /k-s/ is the neatest?

LESSON 10

Objectives

HANDWRITING: Learn the phonogram o.

PHONEMIC AWARENESS: Practice blending sounds into words. Learn to segment words into sounds.

Materials

NEEDED: LOE whiteboard, *Doodling Dragons,* Phonogram Cards learned so far and o, Tactile Card o or o

OPTIONAL: Foods and activities for "o" Day, balance beam or masking tape, Rhythm of Handwriting Quick Reference

Phonemic Awareness

Blending Animal Words

Today I will segment the sounds for an animal. Blend the word back together and pretend to be that animal.

/s-ē-l/	*seal*	/b-er-d/	*bird*
/d-ŏ-g/	*dog*	/f-r-ŏ-g/	*frog*
/k-ĭ-t-ĕ-n/	*kitten*	/k-ow/	*cow*
/p-ĭ-g/	*pig*	/f-ĭ-sh/	*fish*
/h-or-s/	*horse*	/ĕ-l-ĕ-f-ă-n-t/	*elephant*
/m-ŏ-n-k-ē/	*monkey*		

Segmenting Words

10.1 Segmenting Words

You have a page with eight animals.
Segment the name of each animal, and I will guess what you are saying.

Teacher Tip

When students are first learning to segment words, they often will blend two sounds together. Simply restate it with all the sounds segmented and go on. At this point the goal is for students to understand that all words can be segmented. It is not important that they do it perfectly.

/f-ĭ-sh/	fish	*/p-ĭ-g/*	pig
/m-ow-s/	mouse	*/s-ē-l/*	seal
/b-ā-r/	bear	*/ow-l/*	owl
/sh-ē-p/	sheep	*/f-ŏ-x/*	fox

The Phonogram o

The Phonogram o

Today we will learn a new phonogram.

Show the Phonogram Card o.

This says /ŏ-ō-ö/. What does it say? ***/ŏ-ō-ö/***

How many sounds is /ŏ-ō-ö/? ***three***

Let's read all the phonograms we have learned so far.

Phonogram Card o

o Day

Eat omelettes, olives, and okra, and make open faced sandwiches. Find things that open. Learn that *oct-* means eight. Read books about octopi, oxen, ostriches, opossum, and otters. Learn how to draw an octagon. Study the Olympics or the ocean.

Doodling Dragons: Sounds in Words

Today we will read the /ŏ-ō-ö/ page in *Doodling Dragons.*

Point to the phonogram o on the page.

What does this say? ***/ŏ-ō-ö/***

Read the page three additional times as students jump, stand, and shout when they hear the targeted sound.

Doodling Dragons

Phonogram Tight Rope

Direct the student to stand against the wall. Show him a phonogram. Ask him to read the sounds. If he reads it correctly, he may take one step forward. His heel must touch his toe for each step. Then he should write the phonogram in the air. If he writes it correctly he may take another step. When he reaches (chose a location), he wins the game.

Phonogram Cards
Balance beam or
Masking tape

Multi-Sensory Fun

Use a balance beam, or put tape on the floor to make a line to balance on.

Classroom: Phonogram Stop and Go

1) Choose one student to be the "Stop and Go Light." 2) This student will hold a set of all the Phonogram Cards that have been learned so far. 3) Line up the remaining students side by side in a line facing the "Stop and Go Light." 4) When the student with the flash cards turns his back to the students, they must remain still. 5) The "Stop and Go Light" announces how the stu-

Phonogram Cards

dents will move forward. For example: tiptoe, baby steps, giant steps… 6) The "Stop and Go Light" turns around showing a phonogram. 7) The students read all the sounds. For each sound, they can take one step forward. 8) The "Stop and Go Light" turns back around, chooses the next phonogram, and announces how they will move forward. 9) When the students reach the "Stop and Go Light," a new student is chosen to lead.

Handwriting

Writing the Phonogram o

Whiteboard
Phonogram Card o
Tactile Card o or o
Rhythm of Handwriting Quick Reference

Now we will learn how to write /ŏ-ō-ö/.

Demonstrate how to write /ŏ-ō-ö/ using o or o. See page 42 to review how to dictate the steps.

Cursive Only: Show the Phonogram Card o and the Tactile Card o.

What do you notice is different? ***There is a curve stroke at the beginning of the cursive /ŏ-ō-ö/. There is a line at the top of /ŏ-ō-ö/.***

If needed, teach the dip stroke with instructions from the Rhythm of Handwriting Cursive Quick Reference.

This line is how we will connect /ŏ-ō-ö/ to the next phonogram in the word. It is called a dip connector. Most of the phonograms will connect from the baseline. Some of them like /ŏ-ō-ö/ end at the midline and will connect with a dip connector.

①**Curve** around to just below the midline, ②**roll** around past the baseline and back up to the midline, ③**dip** connector at the midline. /ŏ-ō-ö/

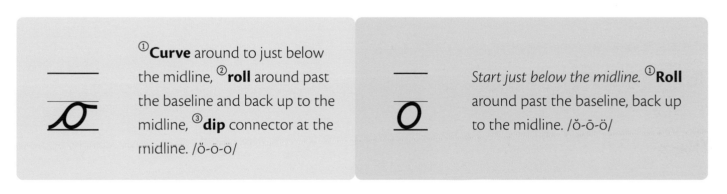

Start just below the midline. ①**Roll** around past the baseline, back up to the midline. /ŏ-ō-ö/

Write /ŏ-ō-ö/ with your pointer finger.

Now write /ŏ-ō-ö/ very large in the air using your arm. Tell me the directions as you write it.

Using a marker, write /ŏ-ō-ö/ on your whiteboard.

Matching Phonograms

10.2 Matching Phonograms

Match the bookface and handwritten phonograms.

Phonogram Practice

Optional Phonogram Aerobics

Phonogram Cards

Practice writing the phonograms with "Phonogram Aerobics" on page 47.

Writing on Paper

10.3 Handwriting Practice

Write /ŏ-ō-ö/ three times on your favorite line size.
Which /ŏ-ō-ö/ sits on the baseline the best?
Which one is the best shape?

REVIEW LESSON B

Area	Skill	Mastery
Phonemic Awareness	Blend one-syllable CVC words.	1
	Blend one-syllable words with a consonant blend.	3
	Blend two-syllable words.	3
	Identify the initial sound in words.	2
Handwriting	Write the down, swing, roll, curve (straight) strokes.	2
	Write the drop-swoop stroke.	3
	Write a.	2
	Write c, d, g, and o.	2/3
Phonograms	Read the phonogram a.	1
	Read the phonogram d.	2
	Read the phonogram g.	2
	Read the phonogram c.	2
	Read the phonogram o.	2

Phonemic Awareness Assessment

Blending One-Syllable Words & Initial Sounds

B.1 One-Syllable Words

Red, blue, yellow, black, and green crayons

I will tell you a color. Pick a crayon that matches. Show it to me. Then I will segment a word. Blend the word back together and circle it with the crayon.

red /b-ă-t/
blue /d-ŭ-k/
green /ă-n-t/

With a black crayon, write an X over the picture that starts with the sound /k/. cow

With a yellow crayon, write an X over the picture that start with the sound /f/. fish

Phonogram Assessment

For the Teacher

Teacher Tip

Choose either Phonogram Slap or B.2 What's That Phonogram? to assess the students' recognition of the phonograms.

There are three levels of mastery when it comes to reading phonograms and words. The first level is to be able to select the written phonogram from a group of choices when the teacher says the sound(s). The second level of mastery is to be able to read the phonogram without prompting. The deepest level of mastery is to be able to write the phonogram upon hearing the sounds. Students should be working toward the deepest level of mastery. At this point in the *Foundations* program, it is enough for students to be able to select the correct phonogram from a group of choices. An optional assessment of writing phonograms will be provided for teachers who desire to measure their student's progress. However, do not prevent students from moving on at this point if they are unable to write the phonograms without prompting.

Phonogram Slap

Lay the phonograms on the table. Tell the student you will call out a sound and she is to slap the phonogram as quickly as possible.

/k-s/
/ă-ā-ä/
/g-j/
/d/
/ŏ-ō-ö/

Phonogram Cards
a, c, d, g, o

Multi-Sensory Fun

Use a fly swatter or a toy sticky hand to play Phonogram Slap.

What's That Phonogram?

B.2 What's That Phonogram?

On your page are groups of four phonograms. I will say a phonogram's sound(s). Color the phonogram with your highlighter.

1. /d/
2. /g-j/
3. /ŏ-ō-ö/
4. /k-s/
5. /ă ā ä/

Highlighter

Phonogram Hop

Lay the phonograms on the floor in a line. Ask the students to jump on each one and read the sound(s). In a classroom, have the students form a line and take turns jumping on the phonograms. Rearrange the order of the phonograms after every third student.

Phonogram Cards

Handwriting Assessment

For the Teacher

At this point, begin to assess students on their ability to write phonograms rather than their ability to write the strokes in isolation.

Teacher Tip

Prompt students with the strokes if needed. Do not expect students to master writing the phonograms. If the student is grasping the rest of the material, move on. There will be plenty of practice in later lessons with writing.

Handwriting

Today I will call out a phonogram for you to write. Write it on your whiteboard (or in the sensory box).

/ă-ā-ä/
/ŏ-ō-ö/
/d/
/g-j/
/k-s/

Whiteboard or sensory box

Multi-Sensory Fun

Fill the sensory box with shaving cream.

Practice Ideas

Blending

Review blending words with the following activities and games:
"Blending Active Words" on page 29
"Blending Treasure Hunt" on page 39
"Blending Animal Words" on page 49

Teacher Tip

For students who struggle to blend one-syllable CVC words, avoid two-syllable words and words with consonant blends. Focus the activity on simple words to build confidence.

Initial Sounds

Chose a set of stuffed animals or other toys. Place them on the table. Tell the student, "I am thinking of a toy that begins with /_/." Direct the student to figure out which toy it is.

This same game can be played with students' names in a classroom.

Phonograms

Review the phonograms with one or more of the following games:
"Optional Phonogram Aerobics" on page 52
"Phonogram Hopscotch" on page 47
"Phonogram Tight Rope" on page 50
"Phonogram Slap" on page 55
"Phonogram Hop" on page 55

Handwriting

Review handwriting with one of the following activities:
"Sensory Writing" on page 43
"Phonogram Aerobics" on page 47

LESSON 11

Objectives

HANDWRITING: Learn the drop-hook stroke.

PHONEMIC AWARENESS: Practice listening for sounds at the beginning of words. Practice blending consonants. Practice segmenting words.

Materials

NEEDED: LOE whiteboard and colored markers, Phonogram Cards, Tactile Card 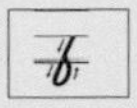 or 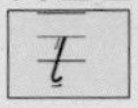 (drop-hook), index cards

OPTIONAL: Toy animals, sidewalk chalk, Tactile Cards or Sandpaper Letters

Phonemic Awareness

Guess the Animal Game

11.1 Guess the Animal

Today I am thinking of a word. It is an animal that begins with the sound /l/. What animal begins with the sound /l/? ***lion***

I am thinking of an animal that begins with the sound /m/. What animal begins with the sound /m/? ***moose***

I am thinking of an animal that begins with the sound /t/. What animal begins with the sound /t/? ***tiger***

I am thinking of an animal that begins with the sound /j/. What animal begins with the sound /j/? ***giraffe***

I am thinking of an animal that begins with the sound /z/. What animal begins with the sound /z/? ***zebra***

I am thinking of an animal that begins with the sound /ow/. What animal begins with the sound /ow/? ***owl***

Challenge

Play "Guess the Animal" without picture references.

Challenge

Encourage the students to think of an animal and tell you the first sound, while you guess the animal they are thinking of.

Multi-Sensory Fun

Use toy animals to play "Guess the Animal."

I am thinking of an animal that begins with the sound /b/. What animal begins with the sound /b/? ***bear***

I am thinking of an animal that begins with the sound /w/. What animal begins with the sound /w/? ***wolf***

Blends

I will say two sounds with a space between them. These sounds do not make a word. Blend them together, then run in a circle around the room saying the blended sound.

/g-r/	***/gr/***
/b-l/	***/bl/***
/s-t/	***/st/***
/f-l/	***/fl/***

Teacher Tip

Many students struggle with consonant blends. Practicing blends auditorily will help prepare students for consonant blends in print.

Segmenting Words

11.2 Segmenting Words

You have a page with eight pictures. Segment each of the words and I will guess what you are saying.

/t-r-ŭ-k/	truck
/k-ar/	car
/h-ow-s/	house
/t-r-ē/	tree
/d-ĕ-s-k/	desk
/p-ĕ-n/	pen
/ch-ā-r/	chair
/b-ī-k/	bike

Teacher Tip

Many students will combine sounds when segmenting. If a student says, /tr-ē/, simply model it correctly, /t-r-ē/, before you choose the picture, then continue with the activity.

Handwriting

Writing the Drop-Hook Stroke

Today we will learn a new handwriting stroke. It is called Drop-Hook.

Show the Tactile Card or . Demonstrate the stroke on the card as you explain the directions.

Whiteboard
Tactile Card or (drop-hook)

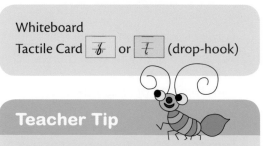

Teacher Tip

Cursive handwriting directions are in the green box. Manuscript handwriting directions are in the blue box.

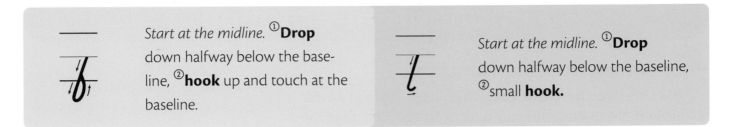

Start at the midline. ①**Drop** down halfway below the baseline, ②**hook** up and touch at the baseline.

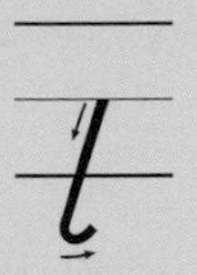

Start at the midline. ①**Drop** down halfway below the baseline, ②small **hook.**

Practice writing the drop-hook stroke with your pointer finger three times.

Write the drop-hook stroke three times on your whiteboard.
Which one is the best? Why?

Point to the stroke you think is the best and explain why.

Writing on Paper

11.3 Handwriting Practice

Write the drop-hook stroke three times on your favorite line size.

Rainbow Writing

Show the students a phonogram. Direct them to read it, then write it on their whiteboard while saying the short directions aloud. The students should then choose a different color and write the phonogram again over the top. Students may choose a third and fourth color to create a rainbow phonogram. Optional: Practice the strokes with rainbow writing as well.

Whiteboard & colored markers
Phonogram Cards
Sidewalk chalk

Multi-Sensory Fun

Create large rainbow phonograms with sidewalk chalk.

Phonogram Practice

Phonogram Treasure Hunt

Tactile Cards or Sandpaper Letters

Hide the Tactile Cards that have been learned so far around the room. Direct students to run and find the hidden phonograms. When they find one, they should bring it to you, "write" the letter, and read the sound(s).

Classroom: Treasure Hunt

Write the phonograms learned so far on 15-20 index cards

1) Divide the class into two teams. 2) Set up 2-4 whiteboards in the front of the room. Choose 2-4 students to check the phonograms. 3) Direct one team to cover their eyes. The second team should hide phonograms throughout the room. 4) The first team then opens their eyes and searches for phonograms. 5) When a student finds a phonogram, he must bring it to one of the checkers, read it, and write it on the whiteboard. 6) If it was read correctly, the checker awards one point. If it was written correctly, the checker awards a second point. 7) Switch the roles of the teams and play again.

Multi-Sensory Fun

Use Sandpaper Letters.

LESSON 12

Objectives

HANDWRITING: Learn the phonogram qu.

PHONEMIC AWARENESS: Practice listening for sounds at the beginning of words. Practice blending consonants. Practice segmenting words.

Materials

NEEDED: LOE whiteboard, Phonogram Card qu, Tactile Card qu or qu, 1-2 sets of Phonogram Game Cards, *Doodling Dragons,* playdough and popsicle sticks

OPTIONAL: Activities for "qu" Day

Phonemic Awareness

Guess the Food Game

12.1 Guess the Food

Today I am thinking of a word. It is a food that begins with the sound /ă/. What food begins with the sound /ă/? ***apple***

I am thinking of a food that begins with the sound /p/. What food begins with the sound /p/? ***pizza***

I am thinking of a food that begins with the sound /w/. What food begins with the sound /w/? ***watermelon***

I am thinking of a food that begins with the sound /b/. What food begins with the sound /b/? ***bread***

I am thinking of a food that begins with the sound /k/. What food begins with the sound /k/? ***cake***
I am thinking of a food that begins with the sound /ī/. What food begins with the sound /ī/? ***ice cream***
I am thinking of a food that begins with the sound /ch/. What food begins with the sound /ch/? ***cherries***
I am thinking of a food that begins with the sound /ĕ/. What food begins with the sound /ĕ/? ***egg***

Challenge

Play "Guess the Food" without picture references.

Challenge

Encourage the students to think of a food and tell you the first sound. Guess which food they are thinking of.

Blends

I will say two sounds with a space between them. These sounds do not make a word. Blend them together, then jump up and down shouting the sound.

/t-r/ ***/tr/***
/p-l/ ***/pl/***
/s-k/ ***/sk/***
/t-w/ ***/tw/***

Teacher Tip

Many students struggle with consonant blends. Practicing blends auditorily will help prepare students for consonant blends in print.

Segmenting Words

12.2 Segmenting Words

Pick a picture. Segment the word. I will guess what picture you are saying.

/b-ä-l/ ball
/t-r-ā-n/ train
/m-oo-n/ moon
/b-ī-k/ bike
/b-ŭ-s/ bus
/k-ī-t/ kite
/s-ŭ-n/ sun
/b-ō-t/ boat

Teacher Tip

Many students will combine sounds when segmenting at this stage. If a student says /tr-ā-n/, simply model it correctly, /t-r-ā-n/, before you choose the picture, then continue with the activity.

The Phonogram qu

Writing the Phonogram qu

Show the Phonogram Card qu.

This says /kw/. What does it say? ***/kw/***

How many letters do we use to write the sound /kw/? ***two***

Many phonograms in English are written with two or more letters.

Doodling Dragons: Sounds in Words

Today we will read the /kw/ page in *Doodling Dragons*.

Point to the phonogram qu on the page.

What does this say? ***/kw/***

Read the page to the students. Read it a second time and ask students to put their finger to their lips each time they hear the /kw/ sound.

Phonogram Card qu

qu Day

Have a quiet time where everyone whispers and tiptoes. Teach students that quart means four. Learn that four quarters make a dollar and four quarts make a gallon. Pour four quarts of water into a gallon jug. Learn about quadruplets, quartz, and quail. Make quilts out of construction paper.

Doodling Dragons

Handwriting

Writing the Phonogram qu

Let's learn how to write /kw/.

Demonstrate how to write /kw/ using qu or qu.

Cursive Only: Show the Phonogram Card qu and the Tactile Card qu.

How is the way we write qu different from how it appears in books? *There is a curve stroke at the beginning of the cursive /kw/. The two phonograms are connected.*

Whiteboard
Phonogram Card qu
Tactile Card qu or qu

Teacher Tip

The qu phonogram has many steps. Be sure to break them down one by one. It is also important for the student to be able to explain each of the steps needed to write the phonogram.

① **Curve** up to the midline, ② **roll** back around to the baseline, ③ **swing** up to the midline, ④ **drop** down halfway below the baseline, ⑤ **hook** up to the baseline, ⑥ touch at the baseline, ⑦ **swing** up to the midline, ⑧ **down** to the baseline, ⑨ **swing** up to the midline, ⑩ **down** to the baseline. /kw/

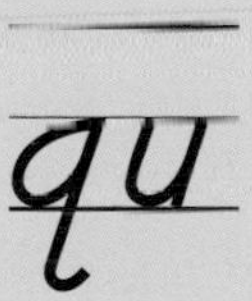

Start at the midline. ① **Roll** around to the baseline, ② **swing** up to the midline, ③ **drop** down halfway below the baseline, ④ small **hook**, ⑤ pick up the pencil, start at the midline, ⑥ **down** to the baseline, ⑦ **swing** up to the midline, ⑧ **straight** to the baseline. /kw/

Practice writing /kw/ three times with your pointer finger.

Write /kw/ in the air with your arm.
Write /kw/ in the air with your thumb.
Write /kw/ in the air with your pinkie.

Using a marker, write /kw/ on your whiteboard four times.
Which one is the best? *answers vary*

Point to the one you think is the best and explain why. Draw a crown next it.

Phonogram Practice

Playdough Writing

Provide students with playdough and a popsicle stick. Have the students roll the playdough out flat and write the phonograms in the dough using the popsicle stick.

Playdough
Popsicle sticks

Phonogram Slap

Place the Phonogram Game Cards that the students have learned face up on the table facing the students. Call out a phonogram's sound(s) and direct the students to race to slap the correct phonogram. If desired, add in a second s reading both the bookface version and the cursive or manuscript version of each phonogram.

1-2 sets of Phonogram Game Cards

Teacher Tip

Students should not be reading from a 90 degree angle. Many young students will develop visual confusion about the letter shapes when asked to read them side-ways or upside down.

Classroom: Phonogram Slap

Divide students into groups of 2-4. Be sure that all the students can read the phonograms right side up. Call out a phonogram's sound(s). Students may race to slap the phonogram. The first one to slap the phonogram takes it.

Writing on Paper

12.3 Handwriting Practice

Write /kw/ three times on your favorite line size.
Which /kw/ sits on the baseline the best?
Which /kw/ has the best shape?

LESSON 13

Objectives

HANDWRITING: Learn the scoop or curve stroke.

PHONEMIC AWARENESS: Learn how to sort vowels and consonants. Practice blending consonants. Practice segmenting words into sounds.

Materials

NEEDED: LOE whiteboard, Phonogram Cards, Tactile Card (scoop) or (curve), whipped cream, plastic plate

OPTIONAL: Phonogram Game Cards

Phonemic Awareness

Vowels: Sounds You Can Sing

Phonogram Cards or
Phonogram Game Cards
a, c, d, g, o, qu
Whiteboard

Today we will test phonograms and put them into groups called vowels and consonants.

The first type of phonogram is called a vowel. It is a sound you can sing and your mouth is open.

Let's test the phonograms we have learned so far and decide if they are vowels.

Show a.

Can you sing the first sound /ă/? */ăăă/, yes*
Is your mouth open as you say the sound? *yes*
Then it is a vowel.

Can you sing the second sound /ā/? */āāā/, yes*
Is your mouth open as you say the sound? *yes*
Then it is a vowel.

Multi-Sensory Fun

Provide students with the Phonogram Game Cards for a, c, d, g, o, and qu. Have them sort the cards into a vowel pile and a consonant pile.

Challenge

Divide the whiteboard in half. Ask students to write vowels on one side and consonants on the other side.

Can you sing the third sound /ä/? ***/äää/, yes***
Is your mouth open as you say the sound? ***yes***
Then it is a vowel.

Show [d].

Can you sing /d/? ***no***
What is blocking the sound? ***my tongue***

So can this be a vowel? ***no***
/d/ is a consonant sound.

A consonant is a sound that is blocked by some part of your mouth, such as your tongue, lips, or teeth. You cannot sing a consonant sound with your mouth open.

Let's test the rest of our sounds and decide if they are consonants or vowels.

Vowels	Consonants
a, o	c, d, g, qu

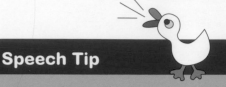

Speech Tip

Some students will mistakenly add the sound /ŭ/ to the /d/ and say /dŭ/ rather than isolating the /d/ sound. In this case they will claim to be able to sing /d/ when in reality they are singing /ŭ/. Help them to hear the difference by singing /ŭ/ then saying /d/ and comparing the two sounds.

Teacher Tip

QU says /kw/. Q always needs a U; U is not a vowel here. It is part of the consonant blend.

Blends

I will say two sounds with a space between them. These sounds do not make a word. Blend them together and march around the room saying the sound they make together.

/s-m/	***/sm/***	/s-w/	***/sw/***
/b-r/	***/br/***	/b-l/	***/bl/***

Segmenting Words

13.1 Segmenting Words

On your page you have eight pictures. Segment each word and I will point to the picture.

/f-or-k/	fork
/s-ä/	saw
/k-l-ŏ-k/	clock
/w-ä-ch/	watch
/b-ĕ-d/	bed
/t-ā-b-l/	table
/b-ŏ-ks/	box
/d-r-ŭ-m/	drum

Multi-Sensory Fun

Practice segmenting words with a Treasure Hunt. Ask one student to segment the word for something in the room, and ask the other students to find the object. When working one-on-one with a student, take turns segmenting and finding the objects so the student can practice both segmenting and blending.

Handwriting

Writing the Scoop or Curve Stroke

Whiteboard
Tactile Card (cursive scoop)
or (manuscript curve)

Today we will learn the scoop (or curve) stroke.

Show the Tactile Card or .

Demonstrate the stroke on the card as you explain the directions.

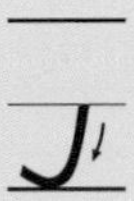

Start at the midline. ①**Scoop** around to the baseline.

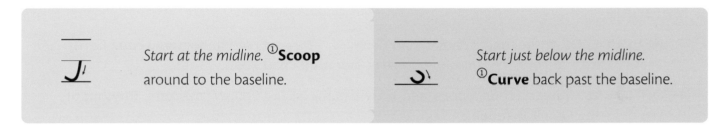

Start just below the midline. ①**Curve** back past the baseline.

Practice writing the scoop (curve) stroke three times with your pointer finger.

Write the scoop (curve) stroke three times on your whiteboard.
Which one is the best? Why?

Point to the stroke you think is the best and explain why. Draw a smiley face next to it.

Writing on Paper

13.2 Handwriting Practice

Write the scoop (curve) stroke three times on your favorite line size.

Phonogram Practice

Phonogram Tic-Tac-Toe

13.3 Phonogram Tic-Tac-Toe

This game requires two players. 1) Assign X's to one player and O's to the other. 2) Direct the first player to choose a phonogram. If he reads it correctly, he may place an X on it. 3) Then the second player chooses a phonogram, reads it, and marks it with an O. 4) The first person to get three in a row wins.

Sensory Writing

Practice writing the phonograms in whipped cream.

Whipped cream
Plastic plate

LESSON 14

Objectives

HANDWRITING: Learn the phonogram s.

PHONEMIC AWARENESS: Review the difference between consonants and vowels. Practice blending consonants. Practice distinguishing vowel sounds in isolation.

Materials

NEEDED: LOE whiteboard, Phonogram Card s, two sets of Phonogram Game Cards, Tactile Card s or s, *Doodling Dragons,* sidewalk chalk, ball

OPTIONAL: Mirror; foods, books, and activities for "s" Day; paper, markers, Rhythm of Handwriting Quick Reference

The Phonogram s

The Phonogram s

Phonogram Card s
Mirror

Show the Phonogram Card s.

This says /s-z/. What does it say? ***/s-z/***
How many sounds is /s-z/? ***two***

Can you sing the sound /s/ with your mouth open? ***no***
Can you sing the sound /z/ with your mouth open? ***no***
Therefore, /s/ and /z/ are consonant sounds.

Put your hand in front of your mouth and say /s/. Can you feel the air coming out? ***yes***

Can you say /s/ with your nose plugged? ***yes***

How long can you hold the /s/ sound. ***/ssssssssssssss/***
What does the /s/ sound remind you of? ***a snake***

Now say /z/. ***/z/***

s Day

Eat spaghetti, sprouts, salami sandwiches, salsa, soup, string cheese, and sundaes with spoons. Make spritz cookies or s'mores. Wear sweaters and socks. Go swimming in swimsuits. Play on a slip and slide. Read books about sailboats, the solar system, Saturn, the sun, spring, summer, or snow. Learn how to sew. Make a scarecrow. Learn about seals and starfish that live in the sea. Explore the senses of smell and sight. Build a snowman.

Compare /s/ and /z/. What is the same about your mouth when you say /s/ and /z/? ***My tongue, teeth, and cheeks are in the same place.***

Why do they sound different?
Put your hand on your throat and say /s/ and /z/. What is different? ***My voice box is on when I say /z/ and off when I say /s/.***

These are related sounds.

Speech Tip

Many young students are missing the sounds /s/ and /z/. Try the following tips to aid the student in producing the sound. Demonstrate how to say the sound using a mirror. First, place your tongue so you can feel the backside of your top teeth. Then pull the tongue back slightly so it is touching the top of the ridge. Lightly put your teeth together. Finally, blow air over the tongue and out the mouth. (For further ideas see *Eliciting Sounds* pages 36-44.)

Doodling Dragons: Sounds in Words

Today we will read the /s-z/ page in *Doodling Dragons*.

Doodling Dragons

Point to the phonogram [s] on the page.
What does this say? ***/s-z/***

Read the /s-z/ page. Reread the page asking students to slither like a snake when they hear the /s/ sound and then zoom like a car when they hear the /z/ sound.

Phonemic Awareness

Consonants and Vowels

Phonogram Game Cards
a, c, d, g, o, qu, s

What do we call a sound that we can sing and our mouth is open? ***vowel***
What do we call a sound that we cannot sing and that is blocked by our mouth? ***consonant***

Read the phonogram. Tell me if it is a consonant or a vowel. How will you decide? ***Test if I can sing it and if my mouth is open.***
If you can sing the sound(s), put it in this pile. This will be the vowel stack.
If you cannot sing the sounds, put it in this pile. These will be the consonant sounds.

Vowels	Consonants
a, o	c, d, g, qu, s

Challenge

Divide the whiteboard in half. Ask students to write vowels on one side and consonants on the other side.

Distinguishing Vowel Sounds

I will say two sounds. Tell me if the sounds are the same or different. If the sounds are the same, whisper, "same." If they are different, shout, "different." Then tell me how your mouth feels different when you say the two sounds.

/ă/ /ă/ *Same.*
/ă/ /ā/ *Different!*
How is your mouth different when you say the sounds? *I pull my mouth back farther to say /ā/.*
/ē/ /ē/ *Same.*
/ĕ/ /ā/ *Different!*
How is your mouth different when you say the sounds? *I pull my lips back farther to say /ā/.*
/ī/ /ē/ *Different!*
How is your mouth different? *My tongue is in a different place and I pull my lips back farther to say /ē/.*
/ŏ/ /ō/ *Different!*
How is your mouth different? *My mouth is round when I say /ō/.*
/ŭ/ /ŭ/ *Same.*

Multi-Sensory Fun

Many students struggle to hear vowel sounds correctly. This activity aids students in feeling how the sounds are different so that they do not need to rely only on hearing the sounds.

Teacher Tip

Some people lower their jaw to say /ī/, compared with /ē/. Others just lower their tongue. Work together with the students to describe how your mouth feels different when you say these sounds.

Blends

I will say two sounds with a space between them. These sounds do not make a word. Blend them together and march around the room saying the sound they make together.

/s-n/	*/sn/*	/f-l/	*/fl/*
/k-r/	*/kr/*	/th-r/	*/th-r/*

Handwriting

Writing the Phonogram s

Let's learn how to write /s-z/.

Demonstrate /s-z/ using Tactile Card s or s.
Use the Rhythm of Handwriting Quick Reference to teach the glide stroke for cursive handwriting, and to review other strokes if needed (swing and scoop for cursive, roll and curve for manuscript).

Whiteboard
Phonogram Card s
Tactile Card s or s
Rhythm of Handwriting Quick Reference

Cursive Only: Show s and .

What is the same and what is different about how we write /s-z/ and how it appears in books? *They look completely different.*

The scoop stroke makes /s-z/simpler to connect within words than if we used the more curvy shape found in books.

Manuscript Only: Some students struggle to form a manuscript /s-z/. Be sure to break down the steps clearly and offer plenty of large motor practice.

①**Swing** up to the midline, ②**scoop** around, ③touch, ④**glide**. /s-z/

Start just below the midline. ①**Roll** around past the midline, ②**curve** back past the baseline. /s-z/

Practice writing /s-z/ two times with your pointer finger.

Write /s-z/ three times large in the air.
Write /s-z/ three times with a marker on your whiteboard.
Which one is the best? *answers vary*

Point to the one you think is the best and explain why. Draw a snake next it.

Matching Phonograms

14.1 Matching Phonograms

Match the bookface and handwritten phonograms.

Teacher Tip

Use every opportunity to refer to a phonogram by its sounds. At this stage do not introduce the letter names.

Writing on Paper

14.2 Handwriting Practice

Write /s-z/ three times on your favorite line size.
Which /s-z/ sits on the baseline best?
Which /s-z/ is the best shape?

Phonogram Practice

Phonogram Memory

1) Mix two sets of Phonogram Game Cards with each of the phonograms taught until this point (a, c, d, g, o, qu, s). Lay all the cards face down in rows in the middle of the table. 2) The first player chooses a card and flips it upright so everyone may see it, and reads the sound(s). He then chooses a second card, flips it upright, and reads the sounds. 3) If the phonograms match, he keeps the pair and goes again. 4) If the phonograms do not match, he returns them to the rows face down and play passes to the next player. 5) The game ends when all the pieces are matched. The player with the most phonogram pairs wins.

Two sets of Phonogram Game Cards in different colors

Multi-Sensory Fun

If you are teaching cursive, use one set of cards with cursive phonograms and one set with bookface. For manuscript, use one manuscript set of cards and one bookface set.

Phonogram Bounce

Outdoors: Write the phonograms with chalk on a driveway or sidewalk. Direct students to bounce a ball onto the phonogram when you say the sound(s).

Indoors: Write the phonograms on large pieces of paper. Direct students to bounce a ball onto the phonogram when you say the sound(s).

Sidewalk chalk
Ball
Paper
Markers

LESSON 15

Objectives

HANDWRITING: Learn the cross stroke.

PHONEMIC AWARENESS: Identify phonograms at the beginning of words. Practice blending consonants. Practice distinguishing vowel sounds in isolation.

Materials

NEEDED: LOE whiteboard, Phonogram Cards, Rhythm of Handwriting Quick Reference or Tactile Card (cross), crackers or chocolate pieces to keep score

OPTIONAL: Phonogram Game Cards

Phonemic Awareness

Phonograms at the Beginning of Words

Phonogram Cards or
Phonogram Game Cards

Today I will say a word. Show me the phonogram that you hear at the beginning of the word. We will only use the first sound of each phonogram.

dog	*The student shows* d.
coat	*The student shows* c.
gate	*The student shows* g.
green	*The student shows* g.
snake	*The student shows* s.
ant	*The student shows* a.
cup	*The student shows* c.
octopus	*The student shows* o.
queen	*The student shows* qu.

Teacher Tip

If the student struggles to select the correct phonogram, limit the student to three choices. Only choose sample words which use those three phonograms. After using all three, then switch to a different set of phonograms.

Challenge

Challenge the students to write the phonogram they hear at the beginning of the word on their whiteboard.

alligator	*The student shows* a.	door	*The student shows* d.
sun	*The student shows* s.	quilt	*The student shows* qu.

Distinguishing Vowel Sounds

I will say two sounds. Tell me if the sounds are the same or different. If the sounds are the same, crouch down low and say, "same." If they are different, jump up and shout, "different." If the sounds are different, tell me what your mouth is doing to make them sound different.

/ŏ/ /ā/ ***Different!***
How is your mouth different when you say the sounds? ***I pull my mouth back farther to say /ā/.***
/ē/ /ē/ ***Same.***
/ĕ/ /ĭ/ ***Different!***
How is your mouth different when you say the sounds? ***I pull my lips back farther to say /ĭ/.***
/ī/ /ē/ ***Different!***
How is your mouth different? ***My tongue is in a different place and I pull my lips back farther to say /ē/.***
/ă/ /ă/ ***Same.***
/ŏ/ /ū/ ***Different!***
How is your mouth different? ***My tongue touches my teeth on the side when I say /ū/.***
/ŭ/ /ŭ/ ***Same.***

Blends

I will say two or three sounds with a space between them. These sounds do not make a word. Blend them together and march around the room saying the sound they make together.

/s-l/	***/sl/***	/s-p-l/	***/spl/***
/g-r/	***/gr/***	/s-t-r/	***/str/***

Handwriting

Writing the Cross Stroke

Whiteboard
Tactile Card (manuscript cross)
Rhythm of Handwriting Quick Reference

Today we will learn the cross stroke.

Use the Manuscript Tactile Card or the Rhythm of Handwriting Quick Reference to demonstrate the cross stroke. Demonstrate the stroke on the whiteboard as you explain the directions.

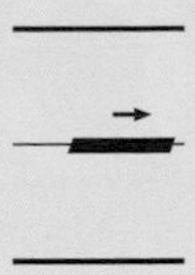

Start at the midline. **Cross.**

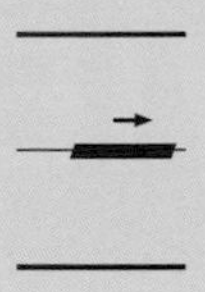

Start at the midline. **Cross.**

Practice writing the cross stroke with your pointer finger.
Write the cross stroke three times on your whiteboard.
Which one is the best? Why?

Point to the stroke you think is the best and explain why.

Teacher Tip

Reinforce that the cross stroke moves in the direction of reading and writing (left to right). When students use this stroke to cross the letter "t" and to write uppercase letters, be sure to emphasize the direction of reading and writing. Also be aware when you are writing on the board to cross your t's in the direction of reading and writing as well. This will help to emphasize directionality and prevent visual confusion.

Writing on Paper

15.1 Handwriting Practice

Write the cross stroke three times on your favorite line size.
Write each phonogram one time.
Which phonograms are the neatest?
Draw a smiley face by your best phonogram.

Phonogram Practice

Phonogram Count

Whiteboard
10 small treats for each student to keep score such as crackers or chocolate pieces

I will call out a phonogram. Repeat the sounds of the phonogram and write it. Each time you get one correct, I will give you a treat. When you have ten, you win, and you may enjoy your treat.

/ă-ā-ä/
/g-j/
/s-z/
/kw/
/d/
/ŏ-ō-ö/
/k-s/

REVIEW LESSON C

Area	Skill	Mastery
Phonemic Awareness	Blend one-syllable CVC words.	1
	Identify the beginning sound in words.	2
	Segment one-syllable CVC words.	2
	Blend two consonants.	2
	Blend one-syllable words with a consonant blend.	3
Handwriting	Write a, c, d, g, and o.	2
	Write qu and s.	3
Phonograms	Read the phonograms a, c, d, g, o.	1
	Read the phonograms qu, s	2

Phonemic Awareness Assessment

Blending One-Syllable Words

Red, blue, yellow, black, and green crayons

C.1 One-Syllable Words

I will tell you a color. Show me that color crayon. Then I will segment a word. Blend the word back together and circle the picture with the crayon.

red /b-ă-g/
blue /b-oy/
green /w-ä-ch/

With a black crayon, write an X over the picture that starts with the sound /j/. ***jar***

With a yellow crayon, write an X over the picture that start with the sound /k/. ***car***

Segmenting Words

Ball
Basket

Set up a basket. Mark a spot from which to shoot the ball. Explain that you will say a word. The student should segment the word and then shoot a basket. In a classroom, the next student then takes a turn.

dog	hat	hit
pit	pat	leg
cat	big	rat
pig	rock	dock
sock	fat	mat
sit	lock	duck

Consonant Blends

Sit in a circle. Roll the ball to the student. Say two consonant sounds, separated. The student should blend the sounds and roll the ball back to you or to another student.

Multi-Sensory Fun

Set up pins. When the student blends the sounds correctly he can roll the ball and try to knock down the pins. Or use a target.

b-l ***bl***	c-r ***cr***	s-m ***sm***
c-l ***cl***	d-r ***dr***	s-n ***sn***
f-l ***fl***	f-r ***fr***	s-p ***sp***
g-l ***gl***	g-r ***gr***	s-t ***st***
p-l ***pl***	p-r ***pr***	s-w ***sw***
s-l ***sl***	t-r ***tr***	t-w ***tw***
b-r ***br***	s-k ***sk***	

Handwriting Assessment

Handwriting

C.2 Handwriting

Choose the line size that you prefer. Write one of each phonogram.

Multi-Sensory Fun

If the student is not ready to write on paper, show the student the phonogram card and have him write the phonogram on a whiteboard or in a sensory box.

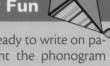

Phonogram Assessment

What's That Phonogram?

C.3 What's That Phonogram?

On your page are groups of four phonograms. I will say a phongram's sound(s). Color the phonogram with your highlighter.

1. /k-s/
2. /d/
3. /g-j/
4. /ŏ-ō-ö/
5. /kw/
6. /s-z/
7. /ă-ā-ä/

Highlighter

Teacher Tip

If the student is able to match the phonogram to its sound(s), he is ready to move on to Lesson 16.

Phonogram Shoot

Attach the phonograms to a wall or whiteboard (a, c, d, g, o, qu, s). Point to a phonogram. Ask the student to read it and then toss a ball or shoot a NERF® gun to hit the phonogram he read.

Phonogram Cards
NERF® gun or a ball

Teacher Tip

Use Phonogram Shoot to evaluate the student's ability to read the phonograms.

Practice Ideas

Blending Words

Review blending words with the following activities and games:
"Blending Active Words" on page 29
"Blending Treasure Hunt" on page 39
"Blending Animal Words" on page 49

Identify Initial Sounds

Review initial sounds with the following activities:
"Guess the Animal Game" on page 57
"Guess the Food Game" on page 61

Segmenting Words

Choose eight to ten objects. Place them on the table. Ask students to choose an object, segment the word, then you will guess the word.

Blending Consonants

Review Consonant Blends by playing:
"Consonant Blends" on page 66
"Consonant Blends" on page 77

Handwriting

Practice writing the phonograms using Sandpaper Letters or Tactile Cards. Hide the phonograms that have been learned so far. Ask students to find them, read them, and "write" the sound(s).

Practice writing the phonograms with the pointer finger using finger paint. Practice writing it with the thumb, and the pinkie finger. Make it fun.

"Rainbow Writing" on page 59

Teacher Tip

Students who struggle with handwriting should practice writing using large motor movements. It is also beneficial for these students to recite the bold, rhythmic directions aloud when writing.

Phonograms

Review the phonograms with your favorite games, including:
"Phonogram Treasure Hunt" on page 60
"Classroom: Treasure Hunt" on page 60
"Playdough Writing" on page 64
"Matching Phonograms" on page 71
"Phonogram Bounce" on page 72

LESSON 16

Objectives

HANDWRITING: Learn the phonogram t.

PHONEMIC AWARENESS: Practice distinguishing vowel sounds. Review segmenting words.

Materials

NEEDED: LOE whiteboard, Phonogram Card t, Tactile Card t or t, *Doodling Dragons*, large whiteboard, NERF® gun with suction cup darts or soft ball

OPTIONAL: Foods, books, and activities for "t" Day, flashlight, index cards, tape, Sandpaper Letters

Phonemic Awareness

Distinguishing Vowel Sounds

I will say two sounds. Tell me if the sounds are the same or different. If the sounds are the same, stand up. If they are different, crouch down. If you cannot decide, repeat the sounds and feel if your mouth is in the same position when you say them.

/ă/ /ĕ/ *Different.*
How is your mouth different when you say /ă/ /ĕ/? ***I pull my mouth back further to say /ĕ/.***
/ă/ /ĭ/ *Different.*
How is your mouth different when you say /ă/ /ĭ/? ***I pull my mouth back further to say /ĭ/.***
/ĕ/ /ĕ/ *Same.*
/ī/ /ī/ *Same.*
/ō/ /ō/ *Same.*
/ŏ/ /oo/ *Different.*
How is your mouth different when you say /ŏ/ /oo/? ***My mouth is rounder when I say /oo/.***
/ĭ/ /ĕ/ *Different.*
How is your mouth different when you say /ĭ/ /ĕ/? ***I pull my mouth back further to say /ĭ/.***
/ŭ/ /ŭ/ *Same.*

Teacher Tip

Some people pull their lips and jaw back to say /ĭ/. Others lower their jaw to say /ĕ/. Work with students to describe how their mouth moves differently to say /ĭ/ and /ĕ/.

I am Thinking of…

One person says, "I am thinking of a ___" and segments the word. The second person finds that object in the room. The players then trade roles.

For example, "I am thinking of a /ch-ā-r/."

Phonograms

The Phonogram t

Show the Phonogram Card t.

This says /t/. What does it say? ***/t/***
Can you sing the sound /t/? ***no***
Is /t/ a vowel or a consonant? ***consonant***

16.1 The Phonogram t

When /t/ is typed in books it can look like any of these on the page. What is the same and what is different between them?

Let the child make observations.

Phonogram Card t

t Day

Eat tomatoes, tabouli, tacos, taffy, tangerines, tater tots, toast, tiramisu, tortillas, tostadas, turkey, tuna, or tofu. Make tents with blankets and tables. Read about turtles, tadpoles, tarantulas, tigers, turkeys, or toads. Visit a dentist to learn about teeth. Take a walk and look at trees. Take a taxi. Play with trains, toys, or trucks. Learn that *tri-* means three. Draw triangles, ride a tricycle.

Doodling Dragons: Sounds in Words

Today we will read the /t/ page in *Doodling Dragons*.

Point to the phonogram t on the page.

What does this say? ***/t/***

Read the page. Re-read the page and ask the students to put their arms in the shape of a T when they hear /t/.

Doodling Dragons

Challenge

Look at the "t" page. Segment a word from the picture aloud. Ask the student to point to the correct picture.

Handwriting

Writing the Phonogram t

Now we will learn how to write /t/.

Demonstrate how to write /t/ using t or t.

Whiteboard
Phonogram Card t
Tactile Card t or t

Cursive Only: Show t and *t*.

What do you notice is different? ***There is a swing stroke at the beginning of /t/.***

①**Swing tall** to halfway between the midline and the top line, ②**down** to the baseline, ③pick up the pencil, ④**cross** at the midline. /t/

Start halfway between the top line and the midline. ①**Straight** to the baseline, ②pick up the pencil, ③**cross** at the midline. /t/

Write /t/ three times with your pointer finger.
Write /t/ in the air.
Write /t/ three times on your whiteboard.
Which one is the best?

Point to the one you think is the best and explain why. Draw a heart next it.

Multi-Sensory Fun

For students struggling with handwriting, use Sandpaper Letters. Help the student to write the strokes in the correct order and say the rhythmic, bold directions aloud.

Writing on Paper

16.2 Handwriting Practice

Write /t/ three times on your favorite line size.
Which /t/ is your favorite?

Multi-Sensory Fun

Write the phonograms on index cards and tape them to the ceiling above the child's bed. Provide the child with a small flashlight. At night have the child light up the desired phonogram and read it.

Phonogram Practice

Phonogram Target

Large whiteboard
Small, soft ball or
NERF® gun with suction cup darts

1) Read the phonogram sound(s) while the student writes them on a large whiteboard to create a target. 2) When all the phonograms have been written, tell the student to step back 3-5 paces. 3) Provide the student with a small, soft ball or a NERF® gun. 4) Read a phonogram. The student should then try to hit the phonogram by throwing the ball or shooting it with the NERF® gun.

LESSON 17

Objectives

HANDWRITING: Learn the phonogram i.

PHONEMIC AWARENESS: Identify the phonogram at the beginning of the word. Practice blending and segmenting.

Materials

NEEDED: LOE whiteboard, all the Phonogram Cards learned so far and i, crayons, *Doodling Dragons*, Tactile Card ī or ī, chocolate chips or tokens for a Bingo game, ball, index cards, playdough, alphabet cookie cutters

OPTIONAL: Foods, books, and activities for "i" Day, Phonogram Game Cards

Phonemic Awareness

Phonograms at the Beginning of Words

Phonogram Cards or
Phonogram Game Cards
Whiteboard

I will say a word. Show me the phonogram you hear at the beginning of the word. We will only use the first sound of each phonogram.

sand *The student shows* s.

goat *The student shows* g.

cup *The student shows* c.

apple *The student shows* a.

dime *The student shows* d.

quick *The student shows* qu.

on *The student shows* o.

game *The student shows* g.

step *The student shows* s.

dive *The student shows* d.

animal *The student shows* a.

Challenge

Ask students to write the phonogram they hear at the beginning of the word on their whiteboard.

Blending Words Together

17.1 Blending

I will segment a word. Blend the word. Find the object on the page.

Then I will segment a color. Use that color to color the object.

/t-ŏ-p/ *top*
/g-r-ē-n/ *green*

/b-ŭ-g/ *bug*
/b-l-ă-k/ *black*

/b-ä-l/ *ball*
/or-ă-n-j/ *orange*

/k-ī-t/ *kite*
/r-ĕ-d/ *red*

/d-r-ŭ-m/ *drum*
/wh-ī-t/ *white*

/b-l-ŏ-k-s/ *blocks*
/b-l-oo/ *blue*

/d-ŏ-l/ *doll*
/p-ĭ-n-k/ *pink*

/b-ā-r/ *bear*
/b-r-ow-n/ *brown*

Crayons

Challenge

Ask the students to choose a picture, segment it, choose a color, segment the color, then color the picture.

The Phonogram i

The Phonogram i

Show the Phonogram Card i.

This says /ĭ-ī-ē-y/. What does it say? ***/ĭ-ī-ē-y/***
How many sounds is /ĭ-ī-ē-y/? ***four***
Let's march around the room two times and recite the sounds as we march. ***/ĭ-ī-ē-y/ /ĭ-ī-ē-y/...***

Can you sing the sound /ĭ/? ***yes***
Is it a vowel sound? ***yes***
Can you sing the sound /ī/? ***yes***
Is /ī/ a consonant or a vowel sound? ***vowel***
Why? ***Because, I can sing the sound /ī/ and my mouth is open.***
Can you sing the sound /ē/? ***yes***
So is it a consonant or a vowel? ***vowel***

Phonogram Card i

i Day

Eat ice cream, Indian food, iceburg lettuce with Italian dressing, Italian food, Italian bread. Go ice skating. Read about igloos, iguanas, and insects. Play with ice cubes. Draw a picture of an island. Find an icicle.

Can you sing the fourth sound /y/? ***no***

So is it a vowel sound? ***no***

That is interesting; /ĭ-ī-ē-y/ has three vowel sounds and one consonant sound.

Doodling Dragons: Sounds in Words

Doodling Dragons

Today we will read the /ĭ-ī-ē-y/ page in *Doodling Dragons*.

Point to the phonogram i on the page.

What does this say? ***/ĭ-ī-ē-y/***

Read the page to the students. Then re-read the page, emphasizing one of the sounds each time. Ask the students to whisper, shout, jump, or clap to each of the targeted sounds.

Handwriting

Writing the Phonogram i

Whiteboard

Phonogram Card i

Tactile Card i or i

Now we will learn how to write /ĭ-ī-ē-y/.

Demonstrate how to write /ĭ-ī-ē-y/ using i or i. Instruct students to write the dot halfway between the top line and the midline.

Cursive Only: Show i and i.

Compare how we write /ĭ-ī-ē-y/ to how it looks in books. What do you notice is different? *The cursive /ĭ-ī-ē-y/ starts with a swing stroke.*

Teacher Tip

Be sure to emphasize the sounds when writing the phonogram. Mastering the four sounds takes a lot of repetition. Hearing the phonogram referred to repeatedly as /ĭ-ī-ē-y/ helps to speed that process.

①**Swing** up to the midline, ②**down** to the baseline, ③pick up the pencil, ④**dot**. /ĭ-ī-ē-y/

Start at the midline. ①**Straight** to the baseline, ②pick up the pencil, ③**dot**. /ĭ-ī-ē-y/

Write /ĭ-ī-ē-y/ three times with your pointer finger on the card. Be sure to say the directions aloud.

Write /ĭ-ī-ē-y/ three times on your whiteboard.

Which one is the neatest?

Point to the one you think is the best and describe why. Put a star by it.

Matching Phonograms

17.2 Matching Phonograms

Match the bookface and handwritten phonograms.

Writing on Paper

17.3 Handwriting Practice

Write /ĭ-ī-ē-y/ three times on your favorite line size.
Which /ĭ-ī-ē-y/ sits on the baseline the best?
Which /ĭ-ī-ē-y/ is the best shape?
Draw a smiley face by the best /ĭ-ī-ē-y/.

Phonogram Practice

Phonogram Bingo

Chocolate chips, or tokens to cover the Bingo squares

17.4 Phonogram Bingo

Using the Bingo Cards provided, call out sounds while the students cover them. Play until the board is covered. Direct the students to read the phonograms back as they uncover each square on the board.

Target Station

Ball
Index cards

Create a Phonogram Target Station. Write the phonograms on index cards and tape them on a blank wall. Have students read a phonogram and toss a ball at it. Award one point for reading it correctly and one point for hitting it with the ball.

Phonogram Playdough

Playdough
Alphabet cookie cutters

Encourage students to cut letters out of playdough and to read the sounds.

LESSON 18

Objectives

HANDWRITING: Learn the circle stroke.

PHONEMIC AWARENESS: Practice identifying phonograms at the beginning of the word. Practice blending words together.

Materials

NEEDED: LOE whiteboard, Phonogram Cards, Tactile Card or (circle), obstacles for an obstacle course

OPTIONAL: Blank paper and clipboard, fly swatter or sticky hand toy

Phonemic Awareness

Phonograms at the Beginning of Words

18.1 Phonograms at the Beginning of Words

Today we will practice listening for sounds at the beginning of words.

You have a worksheet with pictures. Say the name of the picture. Then look at the three phonograms below the picture. Circle the phonogram that you hear at the beginning of the word.

Teacher Tip

For additional practice segmenting, ask students to segment the words on the page before identifying the first sound.

Teacher Tip

If a student struggles to hear the intial sound, repeat the word with the sounds segmented.

Blending Words Together

Challenge

Ask the student to segment the words.

I will segment a word. When you know the word, say it and act it out.

/s-t-ă-n-d/	*stand*
/l-ă-f/	*laugh*
/j-ŭ-m-p/	*jump*
/s-ĭ-t/	*sit*
/h-ŏ-p/	*hop*
/w-ä-k/	*walk*
/s-p-ĭ-n/	*spin*
/r-ŭ-n/	*run*
/s-ĭ-ng/	*sing*
/d-ă-n-s/	*dance*
/t-w-er-l/	*twirl*
/s-m-ī-l/	*smile*

Handwriting

Writing the Circle Stroke

Whiteboard
Tactile Card or (circle)

Today we will learn the circle stroke.

Show the Tactile Card or .

Demonstrate the stroke on the card as you explain the directions.

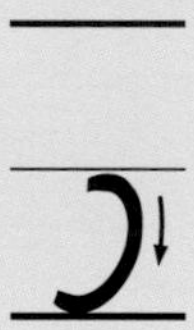

Start at the midline. **Circle** around to the baseline.

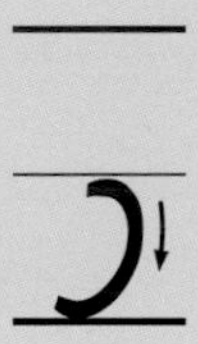

Start at the midline. **Circle** around to the baseline.

Practice writing the circle stroke with your pointer finger.
Write the circle stroke three times on your whiteboard.
Which one is the best? Why?

Point to the stroke you think is the best and explain why.

Writing on Paper

18.2 Handwriting Practice

Write the circle stroke three times on your favorite line size.

Phonogram Practice

Phonogram Obstacle Course

Whiteboard *or blank paper and clipboard*
Phonogram Cards
Markers
Obstacles for obstacle course

Set up nine stations around the room. At each station put a phonogram card and a marker. Between each of the stations place an obstacle to run around, a table to crawl under, something to balance on, or something to climb over. Demonstrate to the students how to go through the obstacle course. Provide each student with a whiteboard or a clipboard with paper. When they see a phonogram, they need to stop, read it, write it on the whiteboard while saying the short directions aloud, and show it to you. When you nod "yes," they can go on to the next obstacle.

Classroom: Obstacle Course

Assign a student referee to each phonogram station. The referee needs to make sure the phonogram is read and written correctly. When one student finishes the course, he then moves into the position of referee for the first station and all the referees move forward one station. This will free one referee to move into the line to complete the obstacle course.

Teacher Tip

Students who act as referees gain a lot of repeated exposure to the phonogram at their station. This is a great way to help students who are struggling with a phonogram to gain additional practice and confidence.

Phonogram Slap

Phonogram Cards
Fly swatter or sticky hand toy

Lay the phonograms on the table. Tell the student you will call out a sound, and he is to slap the phonogram as quickly as possible.

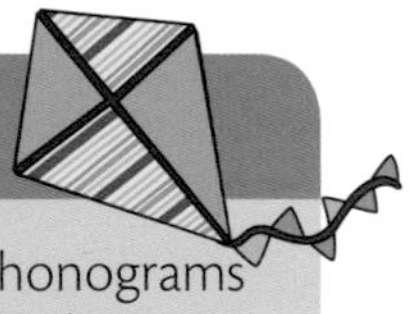

Multi-Sensory Fun

Let the student slap the phonograms with a fly swatter or a sticky hand toy.

LESSON 19

Objectives

HANDWRITING: Learn the phonogram p.

PHONEMIC AWARENESS: Identify the phonogram at the beginning of the word.

Materials

NEEDED: LOE whiteboard, Phonogram Card p, Tactile Card p or p, *Doodling Dragons*, pennies or tokens for a Bingo game, Phonogram Game Cards, stop watch

OPTIONAL: Foods, books, and activities for "p" Day

Phonemic Awareness

Phonograms at the Beginning of Words

19.1 Phonograms at the Beginning of Words

Today we will practice listening for sounds at the beginning of words.

You have a worksheet with pictures. Say the name of the picture. Then look at the three phonograms below the picture. Circle the one that you hear at the beginning of the word.

Challenge

Ask the students to cover the phonograms below the picture. Ask them to say the word, say the first sound of the word, then write the phonogram on the whiteboard.

Blending Active Words

I will segment an action. Blend the word back together, say the word, and do the action.

/k-l-ă-p/	*clap*	/l-ă-f/	*laugh*
/s-ĭ-t/	*sit*	/k-r-ä-l/	*crawl*
/s-p-ĭ-n/	*spin*	/r-ō-l/	*roll*
/h-ŏ-p/	*hop*	/f-r-ē-z/	*freeze*
/f-ä-l/	*fall*	/sh-ow-t/	*shout*
/j-ŭ-m-p/	*jump*	/s-m-ī-l/	*smile*
/k-r-ī/	*cry*	/d-ă-n-s/	*dance*

The Phonogram p

The Phonogram p

Show the Phonogram Card p.

This says /p/. What does it say? */p/*

What is your mouth doing when you say /p/? *My lips are popping. My lips touch and then open.*

Can you sing the sound /p/? *no*

Is /p/ a vowel or a consonant? *consonant*

Phonogram Card p

p Day

Eat pizza, pop, and popcorn. Make a pumpkin pie. Read books about pandas, penguins, pigs, parrots, or puppies. Learn about the Pilgrims and planets. Plant a plant in a pot. Practice counting pennies by plunking them in a pail. Draw a picture with purple pens. Wear pink, purple, or pajamas.

Doodling Dragons: Sounds in Words

Today we will read the /p/ page in *Doodling Dragons*.

Point to the phonogram p on the page.

What does this say? */p/*

Read the page. Ask students to pop up when they hear /p/.

Doodling Dragons

Handwriting

Writing the Phonogram p

Now we will learn how to write /p/.

Demonstrate how to write /p/ using p or p.

Whiteboard

Phonogram Card p

Tactile Card p or p

Cursive Only: Show p and p.

Compare how we write /p/ with how it appears in books. What do you notice is different? *There is a connector stroke.*

①**Swing** up to the midline, ②**drop** down halfway below the baseline, ③slide **up** to the midline, ④**circle** around to the baseline, ⑤touch, ⑥**glide**. /p/

Start at the midline. ①**Straight** down halfway below the baseline, ②slide **up** to the midline, ③**circle** around to the baseline, ④touch. /p/

Practice writing /p/ three times on the Tactile Card using your pointer finger.
Write /p/ in the air with your arm.
Write /p/ in the air with your elbow.
Write /p/ in the air with your foot.

Now write /p/ three times on your whiteboard. Say the short directions aloud and then the sound of the phonogram.
Which one is the neatest? Which circle stroke is the best? Which one sits on baseline the best?

Writing on Paper

19.2 Handwriting Practice

Write /p/ three times on your favorite line size.
Which /p/ sits on the baseline the best? Which one is the best shape?

Phonogram Practice

Phonogram Bingo

Pennies or tokens to cover the Bingo squares

19.3 Phonogram Bingo

Using the Bingo cards provided, call out sound(s) while the students cover the corresponding phonogram. Play until the board is covered. Direct the students to read the phonograms back as they uncover each square on the board.

Speed Writing

Phonogram Game Cards
Stop watch
Whiteboard

1) Provide students with a stack of Phonogram Game Cards (a, c, d, g, i, o, p, qu, s, t). 2) Place the stack of cards face down beside the student. Provide the student with a whiteboard. 3) Start the stop watch. The student flips a card, reads the sound(s), writes it, then flips the next card. 4) Stop when the student has read and written all the cards. 5) Repeat. Can he beat his time?

Teacher Tip

Do not worry about neatness when playing a speed game. If the phonogram is recognizable and the student used the correct order of strokes to write the phonogram, count it. However, if the student writes the c starting at the bottom or changes how the letter is written, ask him to rewrite it.

LESSON 20

Objectives

HANDWRITING: Learn the phonogram u.

PHONEMIC AWARENESS: Practice listening for sounds at the end of the word.

Materials

NEEDED: LOE whiteboard, Phonogram Card u, Tactile Card u or u, two sets of Phonogram Game Cards, *Doodling Dragons*, sensory box with salt or whipped cream or shaving cream

OPTIONAL: Foods, books, and activities for "u" Day

Phonemic Awareness

Listening for Sounds at the End of Words

20.1 Sounds at the End of Words

Today we will listen for sounds at the end of words.

You have a page with six pictures. What do you see on the page? ***cat, bike, cup, fish, dog, house***
I will say a sound. Find the picture that ends in that sound.

Which word ends in the sound /g/? ***dog***
Let's segment the word *dog* and listen for the /g/ sound. ***/d-ŏ-g/***

Now find the word that ends in the sound /sh/. ***fish***
Let's segment the word *fish* and listen for the /sh/ sound. ***/f-ĭ-sh/***

Now find the word that ends in the sound /t/. ***cat***
Let's segment the word *cat* and listen for the /t/ sound. ***/k-ă-t/***

Now find the word that ends in the sound /p/. ***cup***
Let's segment the word *cup* and listen for the /p/ sound. ***/k-ŭ-p/***

Now find the word that ends in the sound /k/. ***bike***
Let's segment the word *bike* and listen for the /k/ sound. ***/b-ī-k/***

Now find the word that ends in the sound /s/. ***house***
Let's segment the word *house* and listen for the /s/ sound. ***/h-ow-s/***

The Phonogram u

The Phonogram u

Today we will learn a new phonogram.

Show the Phonogram Card u.

This says /ŭ-ū-oo-ü/. What does it say? ***/ŭ-ū-oo-ü/***
How many sounds is /ŭ-ū-oo-ü/? ***four***

Let's stomp our feet to the sounds /ŭ-ū-oo-ü/. ***/ŭ-ū-oo-ü/***
Let's clap to the sounds /ŭ-ū-oo-ü/. ***/ŭ-ū-oo-ü/***
Let's jump to the sounds /ŭ-ū-oo-ü/. ***/ŭ-ū-oo-ü/***

Is the sound /ŭ/ a vowel or a consonant sound? ***vowel***
Why? ***I can sing it.***

Is the sound /ū/ a vowel or a consonant sound? ***vowel***
Why? ***I can sing it.***

Is the sound /oo/ a vowel or a consonant sound? ***vowel***
Why? ***I can sing it.***

Is the sound /ü/ a vowel or a consonant sound? ***vowel***
Why? ***I can sing it.***

Phonogram Card u

u Day

Wear ugly clothes or a uniform. Play a ukulele. Learn how to open and close an umbrella. Put a ball under things in the room. Read a book about unicorns. Learn that *uni-* means one. Talk about how a unicorn has one horn and a unicycle has one wheel. Send helium balloons up. Play with toys upside down.

Multi-Sensory Fun

Many students struggle to remember phonograms that have three or more sounds. Take time to move to the sounds. March, clap, jump, roll, stomp, tap... Also say the sounds with rhythm or add intonation.

Doodling Dragons: Sounds in Words

Today we will read the /ŭ-ū-oo-ü/ page in *Doodling Dragons*.

Point to the phonogram u on the page.

What does this say? ***/ŭ-ū-oo-ü/***

Doodling Dragons

Reread the page asking students to listen for each of the targeted sounds. Ask students to jump when they hear /ŭ/, pretend like they are playing a bugle when they hear /ū/, put their hands around the mouth when they hear /oo/, and punch the sky when they hear /ü/.

Handwriting

Writing the Phonogram u

Now we will learn how to write /ŭ-ū-oo-ü/.

Demonstrate how to write /ŭ-ū-oo-ü/ using u or u.

Whiteboard
Phonogram Card u
Tactile Card u or u

Cursive Only: Show u and u.

Compare how we write /ŭ-ū-oo-ü/ with how it appears in books. What do you notice is different?
There is a connector stroke.

Teacher Tip

Be sure to emphasize the sounds when writing the phonogram. Mastering the four sounds takes repetition. Hearing the phonogram referred to repeatedly as /ŭ-ū-oo-ü/ helps to speed that process.

①**Swing** up to the midline, ②**down** to the baseline, ③**swing** up to the midline, ④**down** to the baseline. /ŭ-ū-oo-ü/

Start at the midline. ①**Down** to the baseline, ②**swing** up to the midline, ③**straight** to the baseline. /ŭ-ū-oo-ü/

Practice writing /ŭ-ū-oo-ü/ three times with your pointer finger on the Tactile Card.
Write /ŭ-ū-oo-ü/ in the air.

Write /ŭ-ū-oo-ü/ with a marker on your whiteboard three times.
Which /ŭ-ū-oo-ü/ is the neatest?

Matching Phonograms

20.2 Matching Phonograms

Match the bookface and handwritten phonograms.

Writing on Paper

20.3 Handwriting Practice

Write /ŭ-ū-oo-ü/ three times on your favorite line size.
Which/ŭ-ū-oo-ü/ sits on the baseline the best?
Which one is the best shape?

Phonogram Practice

Texture Writing

Sensory box with salt, shaving cream, or whipped cream

Say a phonogram's sound(s). The student should write the phonogram in the texture using his pointer finger.

Dragon

2 Sets of Phonogram Game Cards
a, c, d, g, i, o, p, qu, s, t, u
Dragon Card

1) Mix two sets of Game Cards together. Deal out all the cards to the players. Some players may have one more or one less card than others. Players should hold their cards in a fan in their hand. 2) Players look through their hand and lay down any matches. As they lay down a match, they must read the sounds. 3) To begin play, the first player chooses another player from whom to draw a card. 4) If a match is found, the sound(s) are read, the match is laid down, and the player takes another turn. 5) If a match is not found, the player adds the new card into his hand. Play then moves to the next player on the left. 6) Play ends when someone lays down all his cards. 7) The player left holding the Dragon card loses.

REVIEW LESSON D

Area	Skill	Mastery
Phonemic Awareness	Identify the beginning sound in words.	1
	Segment one-syllable CVC words	2
	Blend two consonants.	2
	Blend one-syllable words with a consonant blend.	3
	Distinguish consonants as sounds that cannot be sung and that are blocked by some part of the mouth.	2
	Distinguish vowels as sounds that can be sung and the mouth is open.	2
	Identify the final sound in a word.	3
Handwriting	Write qu, s.	1
	Write t, i, p, u.	2
Phonograms	Read the phonograms qu, s.	1
	Read the phonograms t, i, p, u.	2

Phonemic Awareness Assessment

Beginning Sounds and Blending

Green and brown crayons

D.1 Beginning Sounds

Look at the pictures on the page. What do you see? ***gift, table, ant, socks, cake, duck***

Circle the first sound you hear in each of the words.

Give the students time to circle the correct phonograms.

Take out a green crayon. Circle the /g-ĭ-f-t/.

Take out a brown crayon. Circle the /d-ŭ-k/.

Segmenting Basketball

Ball
Basket

Set up a basket. Mark a spot from which to shoot the ball. Explain that you will say a word. The student should segment the word and then shoot a basket. In a classroom the next student then takes a turn.

dad	quit	pat
dog	sit	dip
rod	dig	up
sad	pig	cup
dot	tip	tug
tag	top	jug
cat	pot	rug
it	pit	wig

Blending Basketball

Ball

Sit in a circle. Pass the ball to a student. Say two consonant sounds. The student should blend them and pass the ball to another student.

b-l	c-r	s-l
c-l	d-r	s-m
f-l	f-r	s-n
g-l	g-r	s-p
p-l	p-r	s-t
s-l	t-r	s-w
b-r	s-k	t-w

Handwriting Assessment

Handwriting

D.2 Handwriting

Choose the line size that you prefer. Write one of each phonogram.

Multi-Sensory Fun

If the student is not ready to write on paper, show the student the Phonogram Card and have him write the phonogram on a whiteboard or in a sensory box.

Phonogram Assessment

Phonogram Assessment

Ask the student to read each of these phonograms, using the Phonogram Cards: i, p qu, s, t, u

Phonogram Cards
i, p, qu, s, t, u
Highlighter

What's That Phonogram?

D.3 What's That Phonogram?

On your page are groups of four phonograms. I will say a phonogram's sound(s). Color the phonogram with your highlighter.

1. /kw/
2. /p/
3. /ĭ-ī-ē-y/
4. /s-z/
5. /t/
6. /ŭ-ū-oo-ü/

Teacher Tip

If the student is able to match the phonogram to its sound(s), he is ready to move on to Lesson 21.

Practice Ideas

Sounds at the Beginning of Words

Review beginning sounds by playing:
"Guess the Animal Game" on page 57
"Guess the Food Game" on page 61
"Phonograms at the Beginning of Words" on page 73
"Phonograms at the Beginning of Words" on page 83

Blending Words

Review blending by playing:
"Blending Active Words" on page 29
"Blending Active Words" on page 35
"Blending Words Together: Treasure Hunt" on page 39

Segmenting Words

Choose eight to ten objects. Place them on the table. Ask students to choose an object and segment the word. Guess each word that the student segments.
"I am Thinking of..." on page 81

Blending Consonants

Review Consonant Blends by playing:
"Consonant Blends" on page 66
"Consonant Blends" on page 77

Handwriting

Review handwriting by playing:
"Rainbow Writing" on page 59
"Phonogram Obstacle Course" on page 89
"Texture Writing" on page 96

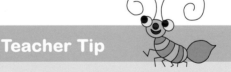

Teacher Tip

Students who struggle with handwriting should practice writing using large motor movements. It is also beneficial for these students to recite the bold, rhythmic directions aloud when writing.

Phonograms

Review the phonograms by playing:
"Phonogram Treasure Hunt" on page 60
"Playdough Writing" on page 64
"Target Station" on page 86
"Dragon" on page 96

LESSON 21

Objectives

HANDWRITING: Learn the phonogram j.

PHONEMIC AWARENESS: Practice listening for sounds at the end of the word.

WORDS: cat, dad, sad, sit, dug

Materials

NEEDED: LOE whiteboard, all the Phonogram Cards learned so far and j, Tactile Card j or j, *Doodling Dragons*

OPTIONAL: Foods, books, and activities for "j" Day, Phonogram Game Tiles, two sets of Phonogram Game Cards

Phonemic Awareness

Listening for Sounds at the End of Words

21.1 Listening for Sounds at the End of Words

Today we will listen for sounds at the end of words.
You have a page with eight pictures. What do you see on the page? ***brush, bug, boat, leaf, car, desk, teeth, crown***
I will say a sound. Find the picture that ends in that sound.

Which word ends in the sound /k/? ***desk***
Let's segment the word *desk* and listen for the /k/ sound. ***/d-ĕ-s-k/***

Now find the word that ends in the sound /t/. ***boat***
Let's segment the word *boat* and listen for the /t/ sound. ***/b-ō-t/***

Now find the word that ends in the sound /th/. ***teeth***
Let's segment the word *teeth* and listen for the /th/ sound. ***/t-ē-th/***

Now find the word that ends in the sound /g/. ***bug***
Let's segment the word *bug* and listen for the /g/ sound. ***/b-ŭ-g/***

Now find the word that ends in the sound /sh/. ***brush***
Let's segment the word *brush* and listen for the /sh/ sound. ***/b-r-ŭ-sh/***

Now find the word that ends in the sound /n/. *crown*
Let's segment the word *crown* and listen for the /n/ sound. */k-r-ow-n/*

Now find the word that ends in the sound /f/. *leaf*
Let's segment the word *leaf* and listen for the /f/ sound. */l-ē-f/*

Now find the word that ends in the sound /ar/. *car*
Let's segment the word *car* and listen for the /ar/ sound. */k-ar/*

The Phonogram j

Writing the Phonogram j

Show the Phonogram Card j .

This says /j/. What does it say? */j/*
Can you sing the sound /j/? *no*
Is /j/ a vowel or a consonant? *consonant*
Place your hand on your throat. Is this a voiced or unvoiced
sound? *voiced*

*I will say a word. If it starts with /j/, do a jumping jack and
say /j/ as loud as you can.*

jump	/j/		smile				
game			jet	/j/		paint	
deer			juice	/j/		desk	
join	/j/		jam	/j/		junk	/j/

Doodling Dragons: Sounds in Words

Today we will read the /j/ page in *Doodling Dragons*.

Point to the phonogram j on the page.
What does this say? */j/*

Reread the page asking students to listen for /j/. Ask students to jog in place each time they hear /j/.

Phonogram Card j

j Day

Drink juice. Eat jam, jello, jerky, and jelly-
beans. Play jumping games. Do jumping
jacks. Jump rope. Tell jokes. Learn about
blue jays, jaguars, and jackrabbits. Watch
a movie about the jungle. Pour water into
jugs and jars. Put together a jigsaw puzzle.
Watch a juggler. Wear jewelry.

Doodling Dragons

Handwriting

Writing the Phonogram j

Let's learn how to write /j/.

Demonstrate how to write /j/using j or j.

Whiteboard
Phonogram Card j
Tactile Card j or j

Cursive Only: Show j and j.

How are these two different? ***There is a connector stroke at the beginning of the cursive /j/. The swoop comes up to the baseline on the cursive /j/.***

①**Swing** up to the midline, ②**drop** down halfway below the baseline, ③**swoop**, ④pick up the pencil, ⑤**dot**. /j/

Start at the midline. ①**Drop** down halfway below the baseline, ②small **swoop**, ③pick up the pencil, ④**dot**. /j/

Write /j/ three times using your pointer finger on the Tactile Card.
Write /j/ very large in the air using your arm. Tell me the directions as you write it.

Write /j/ three times on your whiteboard.
Which /j/ has the best swoop?
Which /j/ has the dot right over the top?
Which /j/ sits on the lines the best?
Put a star next to your favorite one.

Writing on Paper

21.2 Handwriting Practice

Write /j/ three times on your favorite line size.
Circle your favorite /j/.

Phonogram Practice

Moving Phonograms

Phonogram Cards

Say an action. Then show a phonogram card. Ask the student to do the action as he says each of the sound(s).

clap
jump
tap your head
tap your nose
stomp
march
tap your knees
rub your tummy
nod your head
blink your eyes
wiggle your finger...

Optional Matching Phonograms

2 contrasting sets of Phonogram Game Cards: a, c, d, g, i, j, o, p, qu, s, t, u

Provide the student with one stack of Bookface Game Cards and one stack of either Manuscript or Cursive Game Cards. Have the student match the bookface-style letters to the handwriting-style letters.

Words

Spelling List

Whiteboard
Phonogram Game Tiles

Each lesson will include three spelling words plus two challenge words shaded in blue. The teacher should decide how many words to introduce, based on the student's attention span. Use the scripting on the next page to guide you as you teach the spelling words.

Word	Sentence	Say to Spell	Markings	Spelling Hints
1. cat	*The cat is purring loudly.*	kăt	cat	All first sounds.
2. dad	*My dad likes ice cream.*	dăd	dad	All first sounds.
3. sad	*They are sad.*	săd	sad	All first sounds.
4. sit	*Please sit down.*	sĭt	sit	All first sounds.
5. dug	*He dug a hole.*	dŭg	dug	All first sounds.

cat

Today we will learn how to read and spell our first words. We will learn the words by spelling them.

The first word is *cat*. The cat is purring loudly. *cat*

Before we write it, segment the word aloud, just as you have been doing. */k-ă-t/*

I will model how to write it. You will drive my marker by sounding out the word. */k-ă-t/*

As the student sounds out the word, write it on the board.

Teacher Tip

With Logic of English, students spell their way into reading. Once students have learned 10-15 phonograms and have practiced blending and segmenting, they are ready to begin to form words with the phonograms. By beginning with spelling, students construct written words, which helps them to grasp how the phonograms combine together to represent written words.

cat

Watch as I write "cat" again. When do I pick up my marker? ***at the end of the word and to cross the /t/***

cat

When the letters are connected, this means they are working together to form a word. Notice how close the letters sit to one another. As soon as I finished writing one phonogram, I flowed right into the next one. It is like the letters are blended together on the page.

cat

Notice how each of the letters sits close together on the baseline. When they are next to each other, it is the signal to blend the sounds together into a word.

If I were to write them far apart like this:

c a t

then it would look like three phonograms, and I wouldn't know that I should blend the sounds into a word.

Let's read the word together.

Point to each sound.

/k-ă-t/

Erase the board in the direction of reading and writing.

Now it is your turn to write the word *cat*.
Before you write it, segment the word aloud. */k-ă-t/*

The teacher should hold up one finger for each sound as the student sounds out *cat*. Remind students to use /k-s/.

Multi-Sensory Fun

While students sound out the word, it is helpful to hold up a finger to indicate each sound. This provides students with a visual reference of each sound. It also provides a way to indicate multi-letter phonograms in later lessons. For examples, go to www.logicofenglish.com/topics and watch the Spelling Dictation video.

Now segment *cat* again and write each of the sounds on your whiteboard. As you write it, say each of the sounds so I can hear you. ***/k-ă-t/***

The student writes *cat* on her whiteboard.

It is now my turn to write *cat*. Drive my marker by sounding it out. ***/k-ă-t/***

While the student sounds it out, the teacher writes *cat* on the board.

Let's read it together. Point to each phonogram as you read it. Then blend the word together. ***/k-ă-t/ cat***

Teacher Tip

For the first spelling word, cat, the teacher demonstrates how to write letters together to form a word before asking the students to write the word. For the remaining words, the students sound out the word aloud and write it at the teacher's instruction. Then the teacher writes the word as teacher and students sound it out together.

Teacher Tip

At this stage it is more important to keep students engaged and loving learning to read and write than to practice a lot of words. If a student can only write one or two words, respect their attention span. Try writing additional words at a different time of the day. If a student can focus for five, add the challenge words.

dad

The next word is *dad*. My dad likes ice cream. *dad*
Before we write it, segment the word into its sounds. ***/d-ă-d/***

Now segment *dad* again and write each of the sounds on your whiteboard. As you write it, say each of the sounds so I can hear you. ***/d-ă-d/***

Remember to only pick up your marker at the end of the word.

Remember to write the letters so they sit close together on the line and work together to say *dad*.

The student writes *dad* on her whiteboard.

It is now my turn to write *dad*. Drive my marker by sounding it out. ***/d-ă-d/***

The student sounds out /d-ă-d/ while the teacher writes the word on the board.

Let's read it together.
Point to each phonogram as you read it. Then blend the word together. ***/d-ă-d/ dad***

Multi-Sensory Fun

For students who struggle with writing, use Phonogram Game Tiles to practice spelling the target words.

Teacher Tip

In the first few spelling lists no markings or spelling hints are needed, since all the phonograms are saying their first sounds.

sad

The next word is *sad*. They are sad. *sad*
Before we write *sad*, segment the word aloud. ***/s-ă-d/***

Write *sad* on your whiteboard. As you write it, say each of the sounds aloud. ***/s-ă-d/***

The student writes *sad* on her whiteboard.

It is now my turn to write *sad*. Drive my marker by sounding it out. */s-ă-d/*

The student sounds out /s-ă-d/ while the teacher writes the word on the board.

Let's read it together. Point to each phonogram as you read it. Then blend the word together. */s-ă-d/ sad*

Challenge

If the student shows interest, continue with the challenge words. Or dictate challenge words later in the day.

Reading

Matching

21.3 Reading Words

Read the words. Draw a line to match the word and the picture.

Act it Out

I will write a word on the board. Sound it out. Blend it. When you know the word, act it out.

sad *(/s-ă-d/ sad)*

cat *(/c-ă-t/ cat)*

sit *(/s-ĭ-t/ sit)*

dig *(/d-ĭ-g/ dig)*

pig *(/p-ĭ-g/ pig)*

LESSON 22

Objectives

HANDWRITING: Learn the phonogram w.

PHONEMIC AWARENESS: Learn to identify the phonogram at the end of the word.

WORDS: up, pig, pup, sat, it

Materials

NEEDED: LOE whiteboard, Phonogram Game Cards, Phonogram Card w, Tactile Card w or w, *Doodling Dragons,* timer

OPTIONAL: Foods, books, and activities for "w" Day, blocks, playdough, alphabet cookie cutters, Phonogram Game Tiles

Phonemic Awareness

Phonograms at the End of the Word

Phonogram Game Cards
d, g, s, t, p
Whiteboard

I will say a word. Show me the phonogram you hear at the end of the word. We will only use the first sound of each phonogram.

pig	*The student shows* g.
mad	*The student shows* d.
cup	*The student shows* p.
mat	*The student shows* t.
hat	*The student shows* t.
lid	*The student shows* d.
wig	*The student shows* g.
mess	*The student shows* s.
hiss	*The student shows* s.
map	*The student shows* p.

Challenge

Ask students to write the phonogram they hear at the end on the whiteboard.

The Phonogram w

The Phonogram w

Show the Phonogram Card w .

> This says /w/. What does it say? **/w/**

> Can you sing the sound /w/? **no**
> Is /w/ a vowel or a consonant? **consonant**

Doodling Dragons: Sounds in Words

> Today we will read the /w/ page in *Doodling Dragons*.

Point to the phonogram w on the page.
> What does this say? **/w/**

Reread the page asking students to listen for /w/. Ask students to wave each time they hear /w/ in a word.

w Day

Play water games. Eat watermelon, walnuts, water crackers, waffles, walleye, water chestnuts, and wontons. Wear wigs. Ride in a wagon. Show kids a wallet of coins. Find images of George Washington. Go for a walk. Learn about walruses, wallabies, wolves, woodpeckers, or weasels. Go fishing for walleye. Read about the weather. Find worms.

Doodling Dragons

Handwriting

Writing the Phonogram w

> Let's learn how to write /w/.

Demonstrate how to write /w/ using \overline{w} or \overline{w} .

Whiteboard
Phonogram Card w
Tactile Card \overline{w} or \overline{w}

Cursive Only:

Compare how /w/ looks when we write it to how it appears in books. What is different? *There is a connector stroke at the beginning of /w/ and it ends with a dip at the midline.*

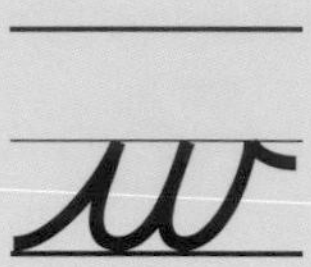

①**Swing** up to the midline, ②**down** to the baseline, ③**swing** up to the midline, ④**down** to the baseline, ⑤**swing** up to the midline, ⑥**dip** connector at the midline. /w/

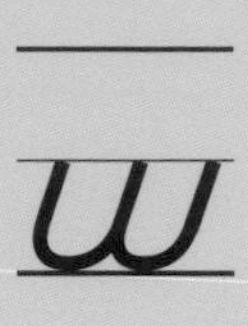

Start at the midline. ①**Down** to the baseline, ②**swing** up to the midline, ③**down** to the baseline, ④**swing** up to the midline. /w/

Write /w/ three times using your pointer finger on the Tactile Card.

Write /w/ three times on your whiteboard.
Which one sits on the baseline the best?
Which one has the same size swing strokes?
Which one looks most like the Tactile Card?
Put a smiley face next to the best /w/.

Writing on Paper

22.1 Handwriting Practice

Write /w/ three times on your favorite line size.
Circle your favorite /w/.

Phonogram Practice

Phonogram Race

Today we will have a phonogram race. I will set a timer for one minute. I will say the sounds of a phonogram. Write it and show it to me. If you write it correctly, I will say the next phonogram. How many do you think you can write in one minute? Then we will do it again and see if you can beat your first score.

Whiteboard
Timer
Blocks

Multi-Sensory Fun

After completing the minute, build a tower using one block to represent each phonogram that was written correctly. Repeat. Compare the heights of the towers.

/ă-ā-ä/	a	/k-s/	c
/ĭ-ī-ē-y/	i	/kw/	qu
/d/	d	/s-z/	s
/g-j/	g	/p/	p
/j/	j	/ŭ-ū-oo-ü/	u
/t/	t	/ŏ-ō-ö/	o

Classroom: Phonogram Race

We will have a race as a classroom to see how quickly we can write the twelve phonograms we have learned. I will say the sound(s) of a phonogram. Write the phonogram on your whiteboards then hold them up. If someone has not written it correctly, I will point. If you did not write it correctly, look around, find the right answer, and correct it. When the whole class is correct, I will read the next one. In this game, you should help each other. If you do not remember how to write the phonogram, look to find hints from others. Remember the class is a team.

Whiteboard
Timer

Teacher Tip

To simplify, limit the number of phonograms to 4-10.

Multi-Sensory Fun

Play the game daily for a week. Keep a running score and watch the times improve.

Words

Review

What do we need to remember about the space between letters when we are writing words?

Only pick up your marker at the end of the word.

I will write a word. Sound it out. Tell me if I wrote it correctly. If I did not, tell me how to fix it.

cat

It is correct. /k-ă-t/ cat

s ad

You picked up your marker between the /s/ and the /ă/. They should be connected.

sad

/s-ă-d/ sad

da d

You picked up your marker between the /ă/ and the /d/. They should be connected.

dad

/d-ă-d/ dad

Write the letters so they sit close together on the line and work together to say the word.

I will write a word. Sound it out. Tell me if I wrote it correctly. If I did not, tell me how to fix it.

cat

It is correct. /k-ă-t/ cat

s ad

There is too much space between /s/ and /ă/. They should be close together.

sad

/s-ă-d/ sad

d a d

There is too much space between the phonograms. They should be close together.

dad

/d-ă-d/ dad

Spelling List

Dictate the words for the students to write on their whiteboards or with Phonogram Game Tiles.

Whiteboard
Phonogram Game Tiles
Playdough and alphabet cookie cutters

Word	Sentence	Say to Spell	Markings	Spelling Hints
1. up	*The books are up on the shelf.*	ŭp	up	All first sounds.
2. pig	*The pig is in the barn.*	pĭg	pig	All first sounds.
3. pup	*The mother dog has one pup.*	pŭp	pup	All first sounds.
4. sat	*He sat on the chair.*	săt	sat	All first sounds.
5. it	*It is hot outside!*	ĭt	it	All first sounds.

up

Today we will write three new words.
The first word is *up*. The books are up on the shelf. *up*
Before we write it, segment the word aloud. */ŭ-p/*
Write *up*. As you write it, say each of the sounds aloud. */ŭ-p/*

The student writes *up* on her whiteboard.

It is now my turn. Drive my marker by sounding it out. */ŭ-p/*

The student sounds out /ŭ-p/ while the teacher writes it on the board.

Let's read it together. Point to each phonogram as you read it. Then blend the word together. */ŭ-p/ up*

Teacher Tip

For students who struggle with writing, use Phonogram Game Tiles to practice spelling the target words.

Multi-Sensory Fun

Provide students with alphabet cookie cutters and playdough. Have the students make the target words with playdough letters.

pig

The second word is *pig*. The pig is in the barn. *pig*
Before we write it, segment the word aloud. */p-ĭ-g/*
Write *pig*. As you write it, say each of the sounds aloud. */p-ĭ-g/*

The student writes *pig* on her whiteboard.

It is now my turn to write *pig*. Drive my marker by sounding it out. */p-ĭ-g/*

The student sounds out /p-ĭ-g/ while the teacher writes the word on the board.

Let's read it together. Point to each phonogram as you read it. Then blend the word together. */p-ĭ-g/ pig*

pup

The next word is *pup*. The mother dog has one pup. *pup*
Before we write it, segment the word aloud. ***/p-ŭ-p/***
Write *pup*. As you write it, say each of the sounds aloud. ***/p-ŭ-p/***

The student writes *pup* on her whiteboard.

It is now my turn to write *pup*. Drive my marker by sounding it out. ***/p-ŭ-p/***

The student sounds out /p-ŭ-p/ while the teacher writes the word on the board.

Let's read it together.
Point to each phonogram as you read it. Then blend the word together. ***/p-ŭ-p/ pup***

Reading

Matching

22.2 Reading Words

Read each word and look at the pictures. Draw a line from the picture to the word.

Challenge

Show students a picture from 22.2. Ask them to write the spelling word which matches it.

Act it Out

I will write a word on the board. Sound it out. Blend it. When you know the word, do the action.

sit ***/s-ĭ-t/ sit***

dig ***/d-ĭ-g/ dig***

pat ***/p-ă-t/ pat***

tap ***/t-ă-p/ tap***

sip ***/s-ĭ-p/ sip***

jog ***/j-ŏ-g/ jog***

LESSON 23

Objectives

HANDWRITING: Learn to connect phonograms with the dip stroke (cursive only).

PHONEMIC AWARENESS: Practice identifying the phonogram at the end of the word.

WORDS: dog, cop, top, pot, pop

Materials

NEEDED: LOE whiteboard, Phonogram Cards, two sets of Phonogram Game Cards including Slap cards, Phonogram Game Tiles

OPTIONAL: Rhythm of Handwriting Quick Reference, sensory tray with shaving cream, whipped cream, or pudding; toy top; picture of a top hat

Phonemic Awareness

Phonograms at the End of the Word

Phonogram Cards
g, d, p, s, t

I will say a word. Show me the phonogram you hear at the end of the word.

log *The student shows* g.

bed *The student shows* d.

bus *The student shows* s.

hat *The student shows* t.

mud *The student shows* d.

bug *The student shows* g.

meat *The student shows* t.

hats *The student shows* s.

flap *The student shows* p.

Handwriting

Connecting Letters with the Dip Stroke

Whiteboard

Rhythm of Handwriting Quick Reference

Cursive Only

Which phonograms have we learned that end on the midline? ***/ŏ-ō-ö/ and /w/***

Today we will learn how to connect phonograms that end on the midline to the next phonogram.

The dip stroke is the connector and /ŏ-ō-ö/ and /w/ are phonograms that connect at the midline.

Multi-Sensory Fun

Have students stand side by side with their feet touching. Most letters connect to one another at their feet. O and W will connect by holding out a hand on one side. The letter next to it will need to lift up one foot to connect. Have one student hold out his hand like the o and the w, and another student lift up his foot to join with the hand.

Watch how I connect /ŏ-ō-ö/ to a /t/. Curve, roll, dip, swing, down, cross.

Say each of the strokes aloud as you demonstrate.

ot

Try writing /ŏ-ō-ö/ connected to a /t/ on your whiteboard. ***Curve, roll, dip, swing, down, cross.***

Now let's connect /ŏ-ō-ö/ to a /d/. Notice how I simply continue from the dip stroke. Curve, roll, dip, small curve, roll, swing tall, down.

od

You try writing /ŏ-ō-ö/ connected to a /d/ on your whiteboard. ***Curve, roll, dip, small curve, roll, swing tall, down.***

Now let's connect /ŏ-ō-ö/ to a /p/. Notice how I simply continue from the dip stroke. Curve, roll, dip, little swing, drop, up, circle, glide.

op

You try writing /ŏ-ō-ö/ connected to a /p/ on your whiteboard. ***Curve, roll, dip, little swing, drop, up, circle, glide.***

Now let's connect /w/ to an /ĭ-ī-ē-y/. Notice how I simply continue from the dip stroke. Swing, down, swing, down, swing, dip, little swing, down, dot.

wi

You try writing /w/ connected to an /ĭ-ī-ē-y/ on your whiteboard. *Swing, down, swing, down, swing, dip, little swing, down, dot.*

Continue to practice og, oc, os, and wo. Refer to the Rhythm of Handwriting Quick Reference to remember the stroke names.

Manuscript Only

When writing words, it is important to write the letters right next to each other. I will write some letters on the board. If they are next to each other, they are a word. Shout, "word!" Then read the word. If they are spread apart, then shake your head, "no."

o t	it	dog	t a p
no	*Word! /ĭ-t/ it*	*Word! /d-ŏ-g/ dog*	*no*

Phonogram Practice

Slap It!

2 sets of Phonogram Game Cards
a, c, d, g, i, j, o, p, qu, s, t, u, w
2 *Slap* cards

1) Deal out all the cards to the players. Some players may have one more card than others. Each player should place his cards in a stack face down in front of him. 2) The first player flips the top card in his stack into the middle so that all players may see it. He then reads the sound(s). 3) The next player flips his top card and places it on top of the card in the middle, and reads the sound(s). 4) If the *Slap* card is flipped, players race to slap it. Whoever slaps the *Slap* card first wins the entire stack of cards from the middle. He then places the cards under his stack and begins the play again. 5) If two matching cards are laid down on top of each other, players race to slap the pile in the middle. The player must then read the phonogram sound(s). If the player does not know the sounds, the other players have another opportunity to slap the pile in the middle and try again. The first player to slap it and read the sound(s) correctly takes the cards. 6) The game is won when one player possesses all the cards.

Matching

23.1 Matching Phonograms

Match the bookface and handwritten phonograms.

Words

Spelling List

Dictate the words for the students to write on their whiteboards or with Phonogram Game Tiles. For an example of spelling dictation, go to www.logicofenglish.com/topics and watch the Spelling Dictation video.

Multi-Sensory Fun

Rather than using a whiteboard, write all the words in shaving cream, whipped cream, or pudding.

Word	Sentence	Say to Spell	Markings	Spelling Hints
1. dog	*The dog chased the cat.*	dŏg	dog	All first sounds.
2. cop	*The cop directed traffic.*	cŏp	cop	All first sounds.
3. top	*It is on the top shelf.*	tŏp	top	All first sounds.
4. pot	*I put the pot on the stove.*	pŏt	pot	All first sounds.
5. pop	*The balloon will pop.*	pŏp	pop	All first sounds.

Vocabulary

Top - Bring a toy top and place it on the top shelf. Place it on top of the table. Show students a picture of a top hat. Demonstrate how top can be used to mean a shirt. Discuss how top can mean "the best" as in the top player. Discuss the different meanings of the word. Ask students to draw a picture for each meaning.

Vocabulary

Cop - In the 1700s and 1800s the word *cop* meant *to grab* or *to catch*. In the mid-1800s it became a slang term for a police officer. Ask students why they think that a word that meant *grab* or *catch* would come to mean a policeman.

Reading

Matching

23.2 Reading Words

Read each of the words on the pages and draw a line to the correct picture.

Practice Spelling

I will say a word. Write it using Phonogram Game Tiles.

sad
top
dad
pig
wig
pup
cop
dog
cat

Phonogram Game Tiles
a, c, d, g, i, j, o, p, qu, s, t, u, w

Teacher Tip

Choose two to nine words depending upon the students' attention span.

LESSON 24

Objectives

HANDWRITING: Learn the bump stroke.

PHONEMIC AWARENESS: Practice identifying phonograms at the end of the word.

WORDS: jug, dig, cup, tap, dip

Materials

NEEDED: LOE whiteboard; Tactile Card 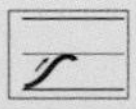 or 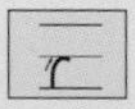 (bump); Phonogram Cards, sensory box with salt, sand, or cornmeal; timer; blocks or LEGO®s

OPTIONAL: Phonogram Game Tiles, die, jug with water and cups, carrots and dip

Phonemic Awareness

Phonograms at the End of the Word

24.1 Identify the Phonogram at the End of a Word

We will practice listening for sounds at the end of words.

Say the name of the picture. Then look at the three phonograms below. Circle the phonogram that you hear at the end of the word.

Teacher Tip

For students who need more help, say the words aloud. Ask them to segment the word and identify the final sound.

bus	mop	rug
hat	bag	ant

Handwriting

Writing the Bump Stroke

Whiteboard
Tactile Card or (bump)

Today we will learn the bump stroke.

Show the Tactile Card or .
Demonstrate the stroke as you explain the directions.

Start at the baseline. **Bump** up to the midline.

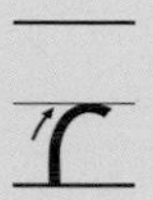

Start at the baseline. **Bump** up to the midline.

Practice writing the bump stroke with your pointer finger three times on the Tactile Card.

Write the bump stroke three times on your whiteboard.
Which one is the best? Why?

Point to the stroke you think is the best and explain why.

Writing on Paper

24.2 Handwriting Practice

Write the bump stroke three times on your favorite line size.
Put a smiley face next to the best one.

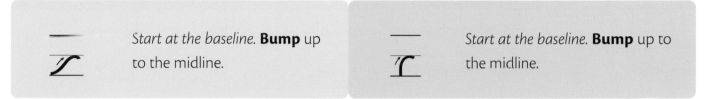

Phonogram Practice

Phonogram Journey

Phonogram Cards
Whiteboard
Die

1) Direct the student to stand at one end of the room holding a whiteboard and dry erase marker. Choose a location in the room as the finish line. 2) Read a phonogram's sound(s). The student should write it on her whiteboard. 3) If it is written correctly, she may take one step toward the finish line. 4) If she writes it incorrectly, she must take one step backward. 5) Continue play until the student reaches the finish line.

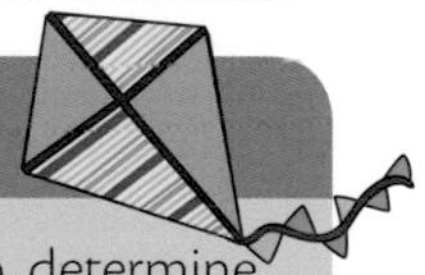

Multi-Sensory Fun

Roll a die with each turn to determine how many steps are to be taken for a correct answer. Take the same number of steps backwards for an incorrect answer.

Words

Spelling List

Dictate the words for the students to write on their whiteboards or with Phonogram Game Tiles.

Multi-Sensory Fun

Write the words in a sensory box filled with salt, sand, or cornmeal.

Word	Sentence	Say to Spell	Markings	Spelling Hints
1. jug	*She bought a jug of milk.*	jŭg	jug	All first sounds.
2. dig	*Use this shovel to dig.*	dĭg	dig	All first sounds.
3. cup	*I need a cup of water.*	kŭp	cup	All first sounds.
4. tap	*Do not tap on your desk.*	tăp	tap	All first sounds.
5. dip	*The dip tastes salty.*	dĭp	dip	All first sounds.

jug

jug She bought a jug of milk. *jug*
Segment *jug*. */j-ŭ-g/*

Write *jug* on your whiteboard. As you write it, say each of the sounds aloud. */j-ŭ-g/*

The student writes *jug* on her whiteboard.

It is now my turn to write *jug*. Drive my marker by sounding it out. */j-ŭ-g/*

The student sounds out /j-ŭ-g/ while the teacher writes the word on the board.

Let's read it together.
Point to each phonogram as you read it. Then blend the word together. */j-ŭ-g/* *jug*

Teacher Tip

If a student uses the phonogram "g" to say the /j/ sound, explain, "You are right, G does say /g/ and /j/. However, G only says /j/ when it is before an E, I, or Y."

Multi-Sensory Fun

Bring a milk jug, a syrup jug, and other jugs to show students. Practice pouring water from jugs into cups.

Vocabulary

Dip - Bring carrots and dip. Discuss the various meanings of dip. Dip can mean a sauce. Dip can be an action. Dip can also mean to take a quick swim.

Salt Box Race

Set the timer for one minute. Say a word. Direct the students to write it in the salt box. Count how many words the student can write in one minute.

dig
cup
jug
dad
sad
cat
pig
pup
dog

cop
top
sit
dug
sat
pot
pop
tap
dip

Sensory box with salt or sand
Timer
Whiteboard

Teacher Tip

In the classroom, students may use a whiteboard for their responses.

Reading

Reading New Words

Once you know the sounds all the phonograms make, you will be able to read any word.

Today we will practice reading words. I will write a word on the board. Each time you read a word correctly, you may add one piece to your building. When all your pieces are built, you win the game.

dad
up
dog
sip
cup
sad
dot
tug
dug
tag
pup
wig
cat

it
quit
did
sit
dig
pig
tip
top
cop
pot
pit
tap

Ten blocks or LEGO®s per student

Teacher Tip

Adjust the number of points based upon the attention span of the student. Also, if a student misses a word, be sure to write it again.

Challenge

Provide the student with 26 blocks. How high can he build the tower by reading words?

LESSON 25

Objectives

HANDWRITING: Learn the phonogram r.

PHONEMIC AWARENESS: Practice identifying phonograms at the end of words. Practice consonant blends.

WORDS: rat, jog, wig, rip, pat

Materials

NEEDED: LOE whiteboard, Phonogram Cards p, s, t, r, Tactile Card r or r, *Doodling Dragons*, two sets of Phonogram Game Cards, Rotten Egg cards, cloth bag, timer, scissors, glue, Reader 1 (in the back of the student workbook)

OPTIONAL: wig, foods, books, and activities for "r" Day, Snatch It! card, Phonogram Game Tiles, crayons, two or three sheets of paper

Phonemic Awareness

Phonogram Cards

p, s, t

Multi-Sensory Fun

Wear a crazy wig. Tell students before their lesson that they will need to figure out why you are wearing a wig.

Blends

Show the Phonogram Card s.

What does this say? */s-z/*

For this activity we will only use the first sound /s/.

Show the Phonogram Card t.

What does this say? */t/*

Hold s and t in each hand so that the students see s on the left and t on the right. Motion for them to read the first sound /s/. Then motion for them to read /t/. Move the cards closer together. Ask them to read each sound closer together. Move them closer again and have the student read each sound. Repeat until the phonograms are next to each other and the students read /st/ blended together.

Show the Phonogram Card s.

What does this say? */s-z/*

For this activity we will only use the first sound /s/.

Show the Phonogram Card p.

What does this say? */p/*

Repeat the activity above until the student reads /sp/.

The Phonogram r

The Phonogram r

Show the Phonogram Card r.

This says /r/. What does it say? */r/*
Can you sing the sound /r/? *no*
What is blocking the sound? *My tongue.*
Is /r/ a vowel or a consonant? *consonant*

Doodling Dragons: Sounds in Words

Today we will read the /r/ page in *Doodling Dragons.*

Point to the phonogram r on the page.

What does this say? */r/*

Ask students to run in place each time they hear the /r/ sound.

Phonograms at the End of the Word

25.1 Identify the Phonogram at the End of a Word

We will practice listening for sounds at the end of words.

Say the name of the picture. Then look at the three phonograms below. Circle the phonogram that you hear at the end of the word.

dress	ship
bat	egg
pear	lamp

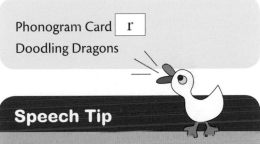

Phonogram Card r
Doodling Dragons

Speech Tip

Many young students are missing the /r/ sound in daily speech. This is one of the most difficult sounds for young students to produce. While demonstrating how to form this sound, draw a picture of the inside of the mouth, including the teeth, palate, ridge behind the teeth, and tongue. Tell the student to touch the tip of her tongue to the ridge just behind the top front teeth. Then pull the tongue back without touching the roof of the mouth. Say the sound using the voice box. If it does not sound strong enough, have the student pull the tongue further back. Be sure to isolate the sound /r/. Be careful to not say /er/ or /rŭ/. (For more ideas see *Eliciting Sounds* pages 91-95.)

r Day

Wear red clothes. Eat radishes, raisins, ramen, ravioli, rice, red peppers, red cabbage, rice cakes, and romaine lettuce. Learn about rabbits. Buy a bouquet of roses. Have a race day. Read books about rabbits, rattlesnakes, race cars, rainbows, roosters, and railroads. Listen to the radio. Visit a pet store to look at rats. Play Red Rover.

Handwriting

Writing the Phonogram r

Let's learn how to write /r/.

Demonstrate how to write /r/ using r or r.

Whiteboard
Phonogram Card r
Tactile Card r or r

Cursive Only: Show the Phonogram Card r and the Tactile Card r.
How is the way we write r different from how it appears in books? ***The top part is straight and not curved. There is a connector stroke to the bottom.***

①**Swing** up to the midline, ②**dip**, ③**down** to the baseline. /r/

Start at the midline. ①**Straight** to the baseline, ②**bump** up to the midline. /r/

Write /r/ three times using your pointer finger on the Tactile Card.

Write /r/ three times on your whiteboard.
Which one sits on the baseline the best?
Which one has the best dip at the top?
Which one looks most like the Tactile Card?
Put a smiley face next to the best /r/.

Writing on Paper

25.2 Handwriting Practice

Write /r/ three times on your favorite line size.
Circle your favorite /r/.

Phonogram Practice

Rotten Egg

1) Place all the Phonogram Game Cards in the bag with the Rotten Egg cards. 2) Set the timer for an undisclosed time of 1-3 minutes. 3) Players take turns drawing a card and reading the phonogram aloud. 4) If a player reads the phonogram correctly, he keeps the card and passes the bag to the next player. 5) If he does not read the phonogram correctly, he must put the card back into the bag and pass the bag to the next person. 6) If a player draws the Rotten Egg card, he must put all his cards back into the bag and pass it to the next player. 7) Play ends when the timer beeps. The player holding the most cards wins.

2 sets of Phonogram Game Cards
a, c, d, g, i, j, o, p, qu, r, s, t, u, w
2 Rotten Egg cards
Timer
Cloth bag
Snatch It! card

Multi-Sensory Fun

Add a Snatch It! card to the bag. If a player draws the Snatch It! card, she may take the cards of any other player.

Words

Spelling List

Dictate the words for the students to write on their whiteboards or with Phonogram Game Tiles.

Word	Sentence	Say to Spell	Markings	Spelling Hints
1. rat	*The cat chased the rat.*	răt	rat	All first sounds.
2. jog	*She went on a jog around the block.*	jŏg	jog	All first sounds.
3. wig	*The clown wore a red wig.*	wĭg	wig	All first sounds.
4. rip	*Rip the paper in half.*	rĭp	rip	All first sounds.
5. pat	*Pat the dog gently.*	păt	pat	All first sounds.

Reading

Reader 1

Reader 1 is located in the back of the student workbook. Tear out the pages of the book and fold in half. Tear out the pages with the illustrations for Reader 1 and set aside.

Today you will read your first book.

Read each of the pages. Then decide if you want to illustrate the book on your own or if you want to cut out the pictures and match them to the words.

When you have finished illustrating the book, read the book to me again so that I can enjoy the illustrations.

Scissors
Glue
Crayons
2-3 sheets of paper

Challenge

Provide the student with 2-3 sheets of paper folded in half to form a booklet. Dictate one word for the bottom of each page. Ask the student to illustrate each word to create a simple book. Or provide the student with a list of words and ask the student to choose which words to include in his book. (dad, dog, sad, gas, dot, tag, cat, cot, sit, dig, pig, top, cop, pot, pit, pat, dip, sip, tap, up, cup, tug, pup, jug, jog, rug, rag, rat, rod, wig)

REVIEW LESSON E

Area	Skill	Mastery
Phonemic Awareness	Identify the ending sound in words.	1
	Segment one-syllable CVC words.	2
	Distinguish consonants as sounds that cannot be sung and the mouth is blocked.	2
	Distinguish vowels as sounds that can be sung and the mouth is open.	2
Handwriting	Write t, i, p, u.	1
	Write j, w, r.	2
	Cursive - Write words connected by a dip stroke. (Many students struggle to correctly connect letters with a dip stroke. Gently and consistently model the correct form and keep moving forward with the lessons.)	2
	Manuscript - Write words with correct spacing between the letters.	2
Phonograms	Read the phonograms t, i, p, u	1
	Read the phonograms j, w, r	2
Reading	Read CVC words.	2

Phonemic Awareness Assessment

Ending Sounds and Blending

E.1 Identify the Phonogram at the End of a Word

Look at the pictures on the page. Circle the last sound you hear in each word. ***bat, glass, bread, net, frog, mop***

I will segment a word. Put an X on it. Put an X on the /f-r-ŏ-g/.

Now circle the word I segment. Circle the /m-ŏ-p/.

Segmenting Basketball

Ball
Basket

Set up a basket. Mark a spot from which to shoot the ball. Explain that you will say a word. The student should segment the word and then shoot a basket. In a classroom, the next student then takes a turn.

dad	quit	pat
dog	sit	dip
rod	dig	up
sad	pig	cup
dot	tip	tug
tag	top	jug
cat	pot	rug
it	pit	wig

Handwriting Assessment

Handwriting

E.2 Handwriting

Choose the line size that you prefer. Write one of each phonogram.

Multi-Sensory Fun

If the student is not ready to write on paper, show the student the Phonogram Card and have him write the phonogram on a whiteboard or in a sensory box.

Phonogram Assessment

Phonogram Assessment

Ask the student to read each of the following phonogram cards: i, j, p, r, t, u, w

What's That Phonogram?

E.3 What's That Phonogram?

On your page are groups of four phonograms. I will say the sound(s). Color the phonogram with your highlighter.

1. /ĭ-ī-ē-y/
2. /p/
3. /j/
4. /r/
5. /t/
6. /ŭ-ū-oo-ü/
7. /w/

Teacher Tip

If the student is able to match the phonogram to its sound(s), he is ready to move on to Lesson 26.

Phonogram Cards
i, j, p, r, t, u, w
Highlighter

Challenge

The ideal handwriting and phonogram assessment would be to dictate the phonogram sound(s) and have the student write it on a whiteboard or on paper without a visual reference. These phonograms may be considered mastered.

Reading Assessment

Reading

E.4 Reading Words

Read the word. Match it to the picture.

Teacher Tip

Encourage the student to try this activity independently. Then listen to the student read the words aloud. In a classroom, listen to each student read 2-3 words aloud.

Teacher Tip

If the student demonstrates an understanding of reading each sound and blending them together, he is ready to move on to the next lessons, even if he is unable to blend the words independently. The next five lessons include extensive practice of blending CVC words.

Practice Ideas

Sounds at the End of Words

"Listening for Sounds at the End of Words" on page 101
"Phonograms at the End of the Word" on page 108
"Sounds at the End of the Word" on page 115

Segmenting Words

Choose eight to ten objects. Place them on the table. Ask students to choose an object and segment the word. Guess the word that the student segmented.
"I am Thinking of…" on page 81

Handwriting

Use the Tactile Cards to reteach how to write any phonograms which students are finding difficult. Break down each step and have the student repeat the short, bold directions aloud.
"Rainbow Writing" on page 59
"Phonogram Obstacle Course" on page 89
"Texture Writing" on page 96
"Phonogram Race" on page 110
"Phonogram Journey" on page 121

Teacher Tip

Students who struggle with handwriting should practice writing using large motor movements. It is also beneficial for these students to recite the bold, rhythmic directions aloud when writing.

Phonograms

"Phonogram Treasure Hunt" on page 60
"Phonogram Slap" on page 64
"Target Station" on page 86
"Dragon" on page 96
"Moving Phonograms" on page 104
"Slap It!" on page 117
"Rotten Egg" on page 127

Reading Words

"Act it Out" on page 107
"Act it Out" on page 114
"Practice Spelling" on page 119
"Salt Box Race" on page 123
"Reading New Words" on page 123

Teacher Tip

At this early stage, expect students to sound out each word, not read it fluently. If the students understand the concept that the letters represent sounds that are blended into words, they are ready to move on. The next lessons will include extensive practice. For students who are not grasping this foundational concept, play some of the Reading Words Games. Point to each phonogram and have the student read the sounds. Then model blending the word together.

LESSON 26

Objectives

HANDWRITING: Learn the phonogram n.

PHONEMIC AWARENESS: Identify the vowel sound heard in the middle of the word. Practice consonant blends.

WORDS: can, and, quit, nut, nap

Materials

NEEDED: LOE whiteboard, all the Phonogram Cards learned so far and n, Tactile Card m or n, *Doodling Dragons,* crayons, markers, or colored pencils, glue, scissors

OPTIONAL: Tactile Card r (straight), foods, books, and activities for "n" Day, two sets of Phonogram Game Cards, two Rotten Egg cards, cloth bag, timer, Phonogram Game Tiles, finger paint and paper, can and can opener, objects for plural practice, index cards

Phonemic Awareness

Vowels in the Middle of Words

Phonogram Cards: a, i, o, u
Phonogram Game Cards: a, i, o, u
Whiteboard

Show the Phonogram Card a.

What does this say? */ă-ā-ä/*

Show the Phonogram Card i.

What does this say? */ĭ-ī-ē-y/*

Show the Phonogram Card o.

What does this say? */ŏ-ō-ö/*

Show the Phonogram Card u.

What does this say? */ŭ-ū-oo-ü/*

Now I will show them to you again. This time read only the first sounds.

Show the Phonogram Card a.

What is the first sound? */ă/*

Show the Phonogram Card i.

What is the first sound? */ĭ/*

Show the Phonogram Card o.

What is the first sound? */ŏ/*

Show the Phonogram Card u.

What is the first sound? */ŭ/*

Today we will practice listening for these sounds in the middle of words.

Multi-Sensory Fun

If a student struggles to distinguish between the vowel sounds, encourage her to repeat the target word, followed by the word that would be formed with the vowel she suggested. Ask her to feel the difference between the words as well as listen to the difference in how they sound.

Provide the student with the Phonogram Cards a, i, o, and u.

If you hear the first sound of one of these phonograms in the middle of the word, hold up the phonogram and show it to me.

dig	jug
fox	win
had	pop
mop	cap
hug	hit
sad	run

Challenge

Ask the student to write on the whiteboard the vowel that is heard in the middle of the word.

Blends

Phonogram Cards

g, d, p, s, t

Show the Phonogram Card g.

What does this say? */g-j/*

Show the Phonogram Card s.

What does this say? */s-z/*

Hold g and s in each hand so that the students see g on the left and s on the right. Indicate for students to look at the s card.

Read this as its second sound /z/.

Teacher Tip

Consonants commonly blend with /s/ and /z/ in plurals such as: *eggs, dads, cats, tops.*

Teacher Tip

S says its voiced sound /z/ after a voiced consonant, such as d or g. S says its unvoiced sound /s/ after an unvoiced consonant, such as p or t.

Motion for them to read the first sound /g/. Then motion for them to read /z/. Move the cards closer together. Ask them to read each sound closer together. Move them closer again and have the student read each sound. Repeat until the phonograms are next to each other and the students read /gz/ blended together.

Repeat the activity above with ds saying /dz/, ts saying /ts/, and ps saying /ps/.

The Phonogram n

The Phonogram n

Show the Phonogram Card n.

This says /n/. What does it say? */n/*
Can you sing the sound /n/? *yes*
But is something blocking the sound? *My tongue is blocking the sound.*
Plug your nose and try to say /n/. Where is the air coming out? *my nose*
Is /n/ a vowel or a consonant? *consonant*
Why? *My tongue is blocking the sound. A vowel is a sound that is open and not blocked.*

Phonogram Card n

n Day

Eat noodles, navy beans, nachos, nuts, naan, navel oranges, nectarines, and neapolitan ice cream. With an adult's help, learn to hammer a nail. Wear a new necklace. Read about nurses, Neptune, narwhals, needle-nosed dolphins, and nuthatches. Learn to count nickels. Find nine night-crawlers.

Doodling Dragons: Sounds in Words

Today we will read the /n/ page in *Doodling Dragons.*

Doodling Dragons

Point to the phonogram n on the page.

What does this say? */n/*

Reread the page asking students to listen for /n/. Ask students to point to their noses each time they hear the sound /n/.

Handwriting

Writing the Phonogram n

Let's learn how to write /n/.

Demonstrate how to write /n/ using m or n.

Whiteboard
Phonogram Card n
Tactile Card m or n
Tactile Card r *(straight)*

Cursive Only: If desired, teach the straight stroke using the Tactile Card r. Compare and contrast it to the down stroke which ends with a small hook.

Show the Phonogram Card n and the Tactile Card m.

What is different between how we write /n/ in cursive and how it is printed in books? *There are two bumps on the cursive version and only one for the print version.*

Look closely at the "n" on the Phonogram Card. Do you see that the letter starts with a straight line? *yes*

In cursive, rather than writing this line straight, we write it as a bump. This makes it easier to write. Also this will help us to tell the "n" and the "r" apart when we are reading cursive.

①**Bump** up to the midline, ②**straight** to the baseline, ③**bump** up to the midline, ④**down**. /n/

Start at the midline. ①**Straight** to the baseline, ②**bump** up to the midline, ③**straight** to the baseline. /n/

Write /n/ three times using your pointer finger on the Tactile Card.

Write /n/ three times on your whiteboard.
Which one sits on the baseline the best?
Which one touches the midline in the right places?
Which one looks most like the Tactile Card?
Put a smiley face next to the best /n/.

Writing on Paper

26.1 Handwriting Practice

Write /n/ three times on your favorite line size.
Circle your favorite /n/.

Phonogram Practice

Choose one activity to practice phonograms.

Whiteboard

2 sets of Phonogram Game Cards, Rotten Egg cards, cloth bag, timer

Blind Writing

Direct the student to close her eyes. Read a phonogram's sound(s). With her eyes closed the student should write the phonogram on her whiteboard. Once she has written it, she may open her eyes. Repeat with a few more phonograms.

Teacher Tip

Blind writing practices the muscle memory needed to write the phonograms. Do not be picky about how each phonogram appears. Rather use the activity to emphasize the strokes.

Optional Rotten Egg

Play "Rotten Egg" on page 127, adding the phonogram n

Words

Spelling List

Dictate the words for the students to write on their whiteboards or with Phonogram Game Tiles.

Word	Sentence	Say to Spell	Markings	Spelling Hints
1. can	*Can you play the piano?*	kăn	can	All first sounds.
2. and	*Run and jump!*	ănd	and	All first sounds.
3. quit	*He quit playing baseball.*	kwĭt	quit	Underline /kw/.
4. nut	*This nut is hard to crack open.*	nŭt	nut	All first sounds.
5. nap	*I need to take a short nap.*	năp	nap	All first sounds.

quit

quit. He quit playing baseball. *quit*

Before we write it, segment the word aloud. ***/kw-ĭ-t/***

Hold up two fingers because /kw/ is a two-letter phonogram.

Write *quit*, saying each of the sounds aloud. ***/kw-ĭ-t/***

The student writes *quit* on her whiteboard.

It is now my turn to write *quit*. Drive my marker by sounding it out. ***/kw-ĭ-t/***

Multi-Sensory Fun

Skip the whiteboards today. Write the words with finger paint.

The student sounds out /kw-ĭ-t/ while the teacher writes the word on the board.

Do you see a phonogram that uses more than one letter? *Yes, /kw/.*

Whenever a phonogram is written with more than one letter, we will underline it to remind us those letters are working together to say one sound. There are two letters, Q and U, working together to say /kw/, so we will underline /kw/.

Let's read it together. Point to each phonogram as you read it. Then blend the word together. */kw-ĭ-t/ quit*

Vocabulary

Can - Bring a can and a can opener. Ask the students, "Can you open the can?" Discuss the two meanings of the word.

Reading

Plurals

Objects to demonstrate plurals
Index cards

I will write two words on the board. Sound them out to yourself and then tell me what is different about them.

cat	cats
/k-ă-t/ cat	*/k-ă-t-s/ cats*

What is the same about these two words? *They both say cat.*
What is different? *One ends in /s/. One means one cat. One means many cats.*
Let's read the next pair.

dog	dogs
/d-ŏ-g/ dog	*/d-ŏ-g-z/ dogs*

What is the same about these words? *They both have the word dog in them.*
What is different? *Dog means one dog. Dogs means many dogs.*

Multi-Sensory Fun

Place the following objects on the table: *maps, dogs, cats, pigs, cups, tags, rugs, pans*. Write the following words on index cards: *map, maps, dog, dogs, cat, cats, pig, pigs, cup, cups, tag, tags, rug, rugs, pan, pans*. Ask the students to arrange the objects and label them.

26.2 Reading Practice

Read the words. Draw a line to the picture that matches.

LESSON 27

Objectives

HANDWRITING: Learn the phonogram m. Learn to leave a space between words.

PHONEMIC AWARENESS: Practice identifying vowels heard in the middle of words. Practice consonant blends.

Materials

NEEDED: LOE whiteboard, all the Phonogram Cards learned so far and m, Tactile Card m or m, Phonogram Game Cards, *Doodling Dragons,* Bingo tokens, highlighter

OPTIONAL: Foods, books, and activities for "m" Day

Phonemic Awareness

Vowels in the Middle of Words

Phonogram Cards and
Phonogram Game Cards
a, i, o, u
Whiteboard

Show the Phonogram Card a.

What does this say? */ă-ā-ä/*

Show the Phonogram Card i.

What does this say? */ĭ-ī-ē-y/*

Show the Phonogram Card o.

What does this say? */ŏ-ō-ö/*

Show the Phonogram Card u.

What does this say? */ŭ-ū-oo-ü/*

Now I will show them to you again. This time say only the first sounds.

Show the Phonogram Card a.

What is the first sound? */ă/*

Show the Phonogram Card i.

What is the first sound? */ĭ/*

Show the Phonogram Card o.

What is the first sound? ***/ŏ/***

Show the Phonogram Card u.

What is the first sound? ***/ŭ/***

Today we will practice listening for these sounds in the middle of words.

Challenge

Direct the students to write on the whiteboard the phonogram that is heard in the middle of the word.

Provide the student with the Phonogram Game Cards.

If you hear the first sound of one of these phonograms in the middle of the word, hold up the phonogram.

pat	lip	rock
bug	sit	pick
pit	sat	stop
lap	mitt	
rug	mutt	

Blends

Phonogram Cards
d, g, p, r, t

Show the Phonogram Card d.

What does this say? ***/d/***

Show the Phonogram Card r.

What does this say? ***/r/***

Hold d and r in each hand so that the students see d on the left and r on the right. Motion for them to read the first sound /d/. Then motion for them to read /r/. Move the cards closer together until you elicit the blended sound /dr/. Repeat the activity above with tr, gr, and pr.

The Phonogram m

The Phonogram m

Phonogram Card m

Show the Phonogram Card m.

This says /m/. What does it say? ***/m/***
Can you sing the sound /m/? ***yes***
But is your mouth open? ***no***

Is /m/ a vowel or a consonant? ***/m/ is a consonant because my mouth is closed.***

m Day

Eat mangos, macaroons, macaroni, maple syrup, marinara sauce, melon, melba toast, matzo balls, mints, mousse, minestrone soup, monterey jack cheese, milk, and museli. Make muffins and malts. Wear mittens and masks. Learn about monkeys, moose, moths, Maltese dogs, manta rays, marsupials, mice, or the moon. Make a maze. Mop the floor. Go to a museum. Make a movie.

Doodling Dragons: Sounds in Words

Doodling Dragons

Today we will read the /m/ page in *Doodling Dragons*.

Point to the phonogram m on the page.

What does this say? ***/m/***

Reread the page asking students to listen for /m/. Ask students to say /m/ and rub their tummies each time they hear the sound /m/.

Handwriting

Writing the Phonogram m

Whiteboard
Phonogram Card m
Tactile Card *m* or *m*

Let's learn how to write /m/.

Demonstrate how to write /m/ using *m* or *m*.

Cursive Only: Show the Phonogram Card m and the Tactile Card *m*.

How is the cursive /m/ different from the one found in books? ***There are three bumps on the cursive /m/ and only two on the bookface /m/.***

Why do you think there would be an extra bump? ***So it doesn't look like /n/. The straight line in the bookface version is written as a bump.***

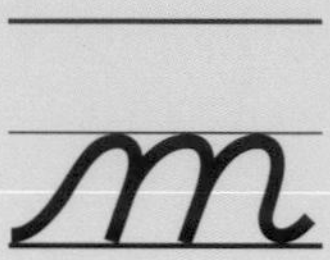

①**Bump** up to the midline,
②**straight** to the baseline,
③**bump** up to the midline,
④**straight** to the baseline,
⑤**bump** up to the midline,
⑥**down**. /m/

Start at the midline. ①**Straight** to the baseline, ②**bump** up to the midline, ③**straight** to the baseline, ④**bump** up to the midline, ⑤**straight** to the baseline. /m/

Write /m/ three times in the air using your pointer finger.

Write /m/ three times on your whiteboard.
Which one sits on the baseline the best?
Which one touches the midline in the right places?
Which one looks most like the Tactile Card?
Put a smiley face next to the best /m/.

Writing on Paper

27.1 Handwriting Practice

Write /m/ three times on your favorite line size.
Circle your favorite /m/.

Phonogram Practice

Phonogram Bingo

27.2 Phonogram Bingo

Pennies, animal crackers, or other game pieces to cover the Bingo squares

Using the Bingo Game provided, call out sounds while the students cover them. Play until the board is covered.

Direct the students to read the phonograms back as they uncover each square on the board.

Reading

Reading Short Phrases

Highlighter

27.3 Reading Phrases

Look at the first line of your worksheet. How many words do you see in this line? *three*

How do you know that there are three words? *There is a space between the words.*

Highlight each of the words. Be sure to leave a space between each word.

Read the first line on your worksheet. */d-ŏ-g/ dog /ă-n-d/ and /k-ă-t/ cat dog and cat*

Draw a line to the picture that matches what you read.

How many words did you read? *three*

How did you know when a word ended? *There is a space.*

Continue in the same manner with the remaining three phrases.

Read and Do

Today we will play a game. I will write a phrase on the board. Read it and then act it out.

sit and pat	run and pat	stomp and pat
run and tap	stand and spin	sit and snap
sit and dig	run and jump	stop and drop

Words

Writing Short Phrases

Whiteboard

When we write words in cursive, all the letters are connected. When we want to start a new word, we pick up our pencil and leave a space as wide as our pointer finger, then begin the new word.

When we write more than one word, we need to leave a space that is as wide as our pointer finger. This space tells us where a new word begins.

Watch how I write three words.

I will sound them out as I write them.

/d-ŏ-g/ Leave a space as wide as my finger. /ă-n-d/ Leave a space as wide as my finger. /k-ă-t/

dog and cat | dog and cat

Now it is your turn to write *dog and cat* on your whiteboard. Be sure to sound out each word and leave a space between the words.

Now write *sad dad.*
What will you write? ***sad dad***
Sound it out as you write it. ***/s-ă-d/ Leave a space. /d-ă-d/***
Now help me to write it. ***/s-ă-d/ Leave a space. /d-ă-d/***

Teacher Tip

The purpose of writing the phrases is for the student to experience the space between the words. Some struggling readers will blend the end of one word with the beginning of the next word. The kinesthetic experience of writing the space between the words helps to emphasize the meaning of the space.

Write the words as the student sounds them out.

sad dad | sad dad

The last phrase is *pots and pans.*
What will you write? ***pots and pans***
Sound it out as you write it. ***/p-ŏ-t-s/ Leave a space. /ă-n-d/ Leave a space. /p-ă-n-z/***
Now help me to write it. ***/p-ŏ-t-s/ Leave a space. /ă-n-d/ Leave a space. /p-ă-n-z/***

Teacher Tip

Some students are not ready to write eight words in one lesson. Rather than asking students to write the phrases, have them drive your pencil by sounding it out and telling you when to pick up your pencil and leave a space.

Write the words as the student sounds them out.

pots and pans | pots and pans

LESSON 28

Objectives

HANDWRITING: Learn the loop stroke or slant stroke.

PHONEMIC AWARENESS: Practice identifying vowels heard in the middle of the word. Practice consonant blends.

WORDS: map, man, mom, gum, tan

Materials

NEEDED: LOE whiteboard, Phonogram Cards, Tactile Card 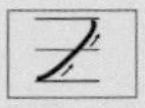 (loop) or 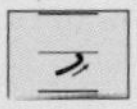 (slant), two sets of Phonogram Game Cards, scissors, glue, Reader 2

OPTIONAL: Phonogram Game Tiles, pudding

Phonemic Awareness

Vowels in the Middle of Words

Review the sounds for each of the vowels with the cards.

Give the student the Phonogram Game Cards.

When you hear the first sound of one of these phonograms in the middle of the word, hold up the phonogram and show it to me.

stump	plan
swim	flap
snap	flip
bump	band
flat	trip
moth	hunt
shop	

Phonogram Cards
Phonogram Game Cards
a, i, o, u

Multi-Sensory Fun

Direct the student to jump up to show the sound. If he is correct he may run one lap around the room.

Blends

Phonogram Cards
d, n, s, t

Show the Phonogram Card n.

What does this say? */n/*

Show the Phonogram Card d.

What does this say? */d/*

Hold n and d in each hand so that the students see n on the left and d on the right. Move the cards closer together until you elicit the blended sound /nd/. Repeat the activity above with nt, and ns, which is pronounced /nz/.

Handwriting

Writing the Loop or Slant Stroke

Whiteboard
Tactile Card (cursive loop)
or (manuscript slant)

Today we will learn the loop (slant) stroke.

Show the Tactile Card or .
Demonstrate the stroke on the card as you explain the directions.

Start at the baseline. **Loop** up to the top line.

Start half-way between the baseline and the midline. **Slant** up to the midline.

Practice writing the loop (slant) stroke three times with your pointer finger.

Write the loop (slant) stroke three times on your whiteboard.
Which one is the best? Why?

Writing on Paper

28.1 Handwriting Practice

Write the loop (slant) stroke three times on your favorite line size.
Circle your favorite one.

Phonogram Practice

Go Fish

2 sets of Phonogram Game Cards
a, c, d, g, i, j, m, n, o, p, qu, r, s, t, u, w

1) Mix two sets of Phonogram Game Cards together. 2) Deal seven cards to each player. Place the remaining cards in the middle of the table face down and spread them out into a "fishing pond." 3) Player A chooses a player (Player B) to ask, "Do you have a __?" Player A should ask for a match to a phonogram he has in his hand, naming the phonogram by its sound(s). 4) If the answer is "yes," Player B must give the requested card to him, and Player A lays the matched cards down in front of him and takes another turn. 5) If the answer is "no," Player B should say, "Go fish." Player A then draws a card from the pond. If a match is found, it is laid down and Player A repeats his turn. If no match is found, play moves to the next player on the left. 6) Play until all the cards have been matched. The player with the most matches wins.

Words

Spelling List

Dictate the words for the students to write on their whiteboards or with Phonogram Game Tiles.

Multi-Sensory Fun

Write the words in pudding.

Word	Sentence	Say to Spell	Markings	Spelling Hints
1. map	*The map is on the table.*	măp	map	All first sounds.
2. man	*A man sat on the bench.*	măn	man	All first sounds.
3. mom	*My mom works here.*	mŏm	mom	All first sounds.
4. gum	*She has mint gum.*	gŭm	gum	All first sounds.
5. tan	*Your tan pants look great.*	tăn	tan	All first sounds.

Teacher Tip

When dictating words, it is important to model the process of segmenting and sounding out words. However, as the students progress, it is equally important to give them increasing ownership of segmenting the words into their sounds. The teacher's role then is to provide clarifications. At this stage, begin to whisper as the student segments the word. Then advance to having the student segmenting the word while you point a finger to each sound. Provide help only when needed or when it is necessary to clarify which phonogram to use, such as C or K for the sound /k/.

Reading

Reader

Reader 2

Scissors
Glue

Reader 2 is located in the back of the student workbook. Tear out the pages of the book and fold in half. Tear out the pages with the illustrations for Reader 2 and set aside.

Read each page. Find the picture that matches. Glue it to the page.

When you have finished, read the book aloud so that I can enjoy the illustrations.

LESSON 29

Objectives

HANDWRITING: Learn the phonogram e.

PHONEMIC AWARENESS: Identify vowel sounds heard in the middle of the word. Practice consonant blends.

WORDS: pen, jet, pet, net, wet

Materials

NEEDED: LOE whiteboard, all the Phonogram Cards learned so far and e, Tactile Card e or e, *Doodling Dragons,* timer, Phonogram Game Cards, scissors, hat or basket

OPTIONAL: Foods, books, and activities for "e" Day, Phonogram Game Tiles, two colors of tempera paint in a gallon-size ziplock bag

Phonemic Awareness

Identify the Phonogram in the Middle of the Word

29.1 Phonograms in the Middle of the Word

Say the name of the picture. Then look at the three phonograms below. Circle the phonogram that you hear in the middle of the word.

bat	pins	bus
hat	rug	box

Blends

Phonogram Cards
m, p, s

Show the Phonogram Card m.

What does this say? */m/*

Show the Phonogram Card p.

What does this say? */p/*

Hold m and p in each hand so that the students see m on the left and p on the right. Move the cards closer together until you elicit the blended sound /mp/. Repeat the activity above with ms, which is pronounced /mz/.

The Phonogram e

The Phonogram e

Phonogram Card e

Show the Phonogram Card e.

This says /ĕ-ē/. What does it say? */ĕ-ē/*

Can you sing the sound /ĕ/? *yes*
Is /ĕ/ a vowel or a consonant? *vowel*

Can you sing the sound /ē/? *yes*
Is /ē/ a vowel or a consonant? *vowel*

e Day

Eat empanadas, elbow macaroni, and eggs. Learn about elephants, emus, egrets, elk, and emperor penguins. Read a book about elves. Dye eggs. Decorate envelopes.

Doodling Dragons: Sounds in Words

Doodling Dragons

Today we will read the /ĕ-ē/ page in *Doodling Dragons*.

Point to the phonogram e on the page.

What does this say? */ĕ-ē/*

Reread the page. Ask the students to listen for /ĕ/ and stand up when they hear it. Then listen for /ē/ and ask the students to lie down each time they hear /ē/.

Handwriting

Writing the Phonogram e

Whiteboard
Phonogram Card e
Tactile Card e or e

Let's learn how to write /ĕ-ē/.

Demonstrate how to write /ĕ-ē/ using e or e.

Cursive Only: Show the Phonogram Card e and the Tactile Card e.

How is the cursive /ĕ-ē/ different from the one found in books? *There is an extra line at the beginning. It is slanted.*

①**Small loop** up to the midline, ②**down** to the baseline. /ĕ-ē/

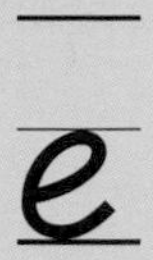

Start halfway between the midline and the baseline. ①**Slant** up to the midline, ②**roll** around to just above the baseline. /ĕ-ē/

Write /ĕ-ē/ three times in the air using your pointer finger on the Tactile Card.

Write /ĕ-ē/ three times on your whiteboard.
Which /ĕ-ē/ sits on the baseline the best?
Which /ĕ-ē/ touches the midline in the right place?
Which /ĕ-ē/ looks most like the Tactile Card?
Put a star next to the best /ĕ-ē/.

Teacher Tip

Notice that /ĕ-ē/ uses a small loop up to the midline.

Writing on Paper

29.2 Handwriting Practice

Write /ĕ-ē/ three times on your favorite line size.
Put a star next to your favorite /ĕ-ē/.

Phonogram Practice

Snatch the Phonogram

1) Place a pile of Phonogram Game Cards at one end of the room. Designate a starting line on the opposite side of the room. Place a whiteboard at the starting line. 2) Read a phonogram's sound(s). 3) The student must write it on the whiteboard, run to the other side of the room, find the phonogram in the pile, and run back. 4) Time the student on writing and finding five to ten phonograms.

Whiteboard
Timer
Phonogram Game Cards
a, c, d, e, g, i, j, m, n, o, p, qu, r, s, t, u, w

Words

Spelling List

Dictate the words as the students write them on their whiteboards or form them with Phonogram Game Tiles.

Multi-Sensory Fun

Put two colors of tempera paint in a gallon-size ziplock bag. Write the words on the bag.

Word	Sentence	Say to Spell	Markings	Spelling Hints
1. pen	*Write the word with a pen..*	pĕn	pen	All first sounds.
2. jet	*A jet flew overhead.*	jĕt	jet	All first sounds.
3. pet	*We have a pet dog.*	pĕt	pet	All first sounds.
4. net	*We caught a butterfly in the net.*	nĕt	net	All first sounds.
5. wet	*My socks are wet.*	wĕt	wet	All first sounds.

Teacher Tip

Whisper as the student segments the word. Provide help only when needed or when it is necessary to clarify which phonogram to use, such as J not G in jet.

Reading

Read and Do

29.3 Read and Do

Cut out each of the words in your workbook. We will fold them and put them into a hat. Choose a word, read it, and act it out.

Scissors

Hat or basket

Challenge

Ask the student to choose two or three words, read them, then act them all out at one time.

LESSON 30

Objectives

HANDWRITING: Learn the phonogram l.

PHONEMIC AWARENESS: Listen for vowels. Practice consonant blends.

WORDS: quilt, log, men, mad, leg

Materials

NEEDED: LOE whiteboard, Phonogram Cards l and t, Tactile Card l or l, *Doodling Dragons,* timer, Phonogram Game Cards; large blank whiteboard and colored dry erase markers, or sidewalk chalk and sidewalk, or large piece of white paper and finger paints; glue, scissors, Reader 3

OPTIONAL: Foods and activities for "l" Day, music, Phonogram Game Tiles, *The Keeping Quilt* by Patricia Polacco

The Phonogram l

The Phonogram l

Show the Phonogram Card l.

This says /l/. What does it say? */l/*
Can you sing the sound /l/? *yes*
What is blocking the sound? *my tongue*
Is /l/ a vowel or a consonant? *consonant*
Why? *It is blocked by my tongue.*

Phonogram Card l

l Day

Drink lemonade. Eat lima beans, lentils, lemon poppyseed muffins, lasagna, lollipops, and licorice. Make paper lanterns.

Doodling Dragons: Sounds in Words

Doodling Dragons

Today we will read the /l/ page in *Doodling Dragons.*

Point to the phonogram l on the page.

What does this say? */l/*

Reread the page. Ask the students to leap when they hear the /l/ sound.

Handwriting

Writing the Phonogram l

Whiteboard
Phonogram Card l
Tactile Card l or l

Let's learn how to write /l/.

Demonstrate how to write /l/ using l or l.

Cursive Only: Show the Phonogram Card l and the Tactile Card l.

How is the cursive /l/ different from the bookface one? *The cursive /l/ is more slanted. There is a loop stroke at the beginning.*

① **Loop** up to the top line, ② **down** to the baseline. /l/

Start at the top line. ① **Straight** to the baseline. /l/

Write /l/ three times using your pointer finger on the Tactile Card.

Write /l/ three times on your whiteboard.
Which /l/ sits on the baseline the best?
Which /l/ touches the top line?
Which /l/ looks most like the Tactile Card?
Put a star next to the best /l/.

Writing on Paper

30.1 Handwriting Practice

Write /l/ three times on your favorite line size.

Phonemic Awareness

Phonograms in the Middle of the Word

30.2 Phonograms in the Middle of the Word

Say the name of the picture. Then look at the three phonograms below. Circle the phonogram that you hear in the middle of the word.

lamp	gum	lock
net	fish	plug

Blends

Phonogram Cards
l, t

Show the Phonogram Card | l |.

What does this say? /l/

Show the Phonogram Card | t |.

What does this say? /t/

Hold them next to one another | l | t |.

What do they say together? /lt/

Phonogram Practice

Choose one activity to practice phonograms.

Phonogram Aerobics

Call a phonogram for the student to write in the air. For example:

Write /s-z/ with your elbow. Write /t/ with your foot...

Multi-Sensory Fun

Turn on music while writing the phonograms in the air.

Snatch the Phonogram

Play "Snatch the Phonogram" on page 151.

Whiteboard
Timer
Phonogram Game Cards
a, c, d, e, g, i, j, l, m, n, o, p, qu, r, s, t, u, w

Words

Spelling List

Dictate the words for the students to write on their whiteboards or with Phonogram Game Tiles.

Word	Sentence	Say to Spell	Markings	Spelling Hints
1. quilt	*The warm quilt is on my bed.*	kwĭlt	quilt	Underline /kw/.
2. log	*Ethan sat on the log.*	lŏg	log	All first sounds.
3. men	*The men worked all night.*	mĕn	men	All first sounds.
4. mad	*Please do not be mad.*	măd	mad	All first sounds.
5. leg	*She hurt her leg.*	lĕg	leg	All first sounds.

Teacher Tip

This list will begin to teach blends. If the student is struggling to segment or read words with blends, review each word with Phonogram Game Tiles, bringing the consonants closer together and saying each sound with less and less space until the sounds are blended. Some students need extensive practice before mastering blends. Further games will be provided in Lessons 31-40.

quilt

quilt. The warm quilt is on my bed. *quilt*
Before we write it, segment the word aloud. ***/kw-ĭ-l-t/***

Write *quilt*. As you write it, say each of the sounds aloud. ***/kw-ĭ-l-t/***

The student writes *quilt* on her whiteboard.

It is now my turn to write *quilt*. Drive my marker by sounding it out. ***/kw-ĭ-l-t/***

The student sounds out /kw-ĭ-l-t/ while the teacher writes the word on the board.

Do you see two letters working together to make one phonogram? ***/kw/***
Let's underline the /kw/ to remind ourselves that the Q and U work together to say /kw/.

Let's read the word together. Point to each phonogram as you read it. ***/kw-ĭ-l-t/ quilt***

Reading

Word Quilt

Read a word. The students write it in any color they desire, any place on a large whiteboard, sidewalk, or paper. (If students are using finger paints, encourage them to write with their pointer finger.) Allow students to write words big, small, sideways, etc. Encourage them to sound out the word. Be gentle with mistakes. Create a love for writing and words.

Whiteboard
Colored dry-erase markers
Sidewalk chalk
Large piece of paper
Finger paints

Book List

The Keeping Quilt
by Patricia Polacco

Read *The Keeping Quilt* aloud to students.

man
dad
dog
sad
gas
cat
cot
it
did
sit
dig
gum
pat
pet
up
cup
jog
rug
wig
sun
run
tan
men
red
map
net
jet
wet

Reader

Reader 3

Read each page. Find the picture that matches. Glue it to the page.

When you have finished, read the book aloud so that I can enjoy the illustrations.

Scissors
Glue

REVIEW LESSON F

Area	Skill	Mastery
Phonemic Awareness	Identify the vowel in the middle of the word.	2
	Segment one-syllable CVC words.	2
Handwriting	Write j, w, r.	1
	Write n, m, e, l.	2
Phonograms	Read the phonograms j, w, r.	1
	Read the phonograms n, m, e, l.	2
Reading	Read CVC words.	2
	Read one-syllable words with consonant blends.	3

Phonemic Awareness Assessment

Medial Sounds and Segmenting

F.1 Phonograms in the Middle of the Word

Look at the pictures on the page. Circle the vowel you hear in the middle of each word. *desk, net, pig, map, sun, log*

Segment one of the words for me. I will point to the one you segment.

Teacher Tip

Many students struggle to distinguish vowel sounds. Encourage students to feel the difference between the sounds. This skill will take time to develop in some students. Continue to Lessons 31-40 as long as the student understands the concept.

Handwriting Assessment

Handwriting

F.2 Handwriting

Choose the line size that you prefer. Write one of each phonogram.

Multi-Sensory Fun

If the student is not ready to write on paper, show the student the Phonogram Card and have him write the phonogram on a whiteboard or in a sensory box.

Phonogram Assessment

Phonogram Assessment

Ask the student to read each of the following Phonogram Cards: e, j, l, m, n, r, w

Phonogram Cards
e, j, l, m, n, r, w
Highlighter

What's That Phonogram?

F.3 What's That Phonogram?

On your page are groups of four phonograms. I will say a phonogram's sound(s). Color the phonogram with your highlighter.

1. /ĕ-ē/
2. /l/
3. /j/
4. /r/
5. /m/
6. /w/
7. /n/

Challenge

The ideal handwriting and phonogram assessment would be to dictate the phonogram sound(s) and have the student write it on a whiteboard or on paper without a visual reference. These phonograms may be considered mastered.

Reading Assessment

Reading

F.4 Reading

Read the word. Match it to the picture.

Teacher Tip

Encourage the student to try this activity independently. Then listen to the student read the words aloud. In a classroom, listen to each student read one phrase.

Practice Ideas

Vowels in the Middle of Words

"Vowels in the Middle of Words" on page 133
"Listening for Vowels in the Middle of Words" on page 139

Segmenting Words

Students practice segmenting with each spelling list. One mistake many teachers make is segmenting the word for the students. Though modeling is important in the beginning, segmenting is the basis of reading and spelling. If the student is struggling with segmenting, in future lessons whisper as the student segments the word. Then ask the student to segment it alone before he writes it.

"I am Thinking of..." on page 81

Handwriting

Reteach how to write any of the phonograms that are difficult, using the Tactile Cards. Break down each step and have the student repeat the short, bold directions aloud.

"Phonogram Obstacle Course" on page 89
"Texture Writing" on page 97
"Phonogram Journey" on page 121
"Blind Writing" on page 137
"Snatch the Phonogram" on page 155
"Word Quilt" on page 157

Teacher Tip

Students who struggle with handwriting should practice writing using large motor movements. It is also beneficial for these students to recite the bold, rhythmic directions aloud when writing.

Phonograms

"Target Station" on page 86
"Dragon" on page 97
"Slap It!" on page 117
"Rotten Egg" on page 127
"Go Fish" on page 147
"Snatch the Phonogram" on page 151

Reading Words

"Act it Out" on page 107
"Act it Out" on page 114
"Practice Spelling" on page 119
"Salt Box Race" on page 123
"Reading New Words" on page 123
"Read and Do" on page 143

Teacher Tip

Reading at this stage is often still choppy. Later lessons will focus on reading fluency. Students are ready to move to Lessons 31-40 as long as they are reading phonogram sounds correctly and attempting to blend them into words. Frequently, students who are struggling to read words need more phonogram practice. Use the review activities listed on this page.

LESSON 31

Objectives

HANDWRITING: Learn the phonogram b.

PHONEMIC AWARENESS: Match the initial sounds of words to the phonogram. Practice blends.

WORDS: big, sand, ran, bad, bend

Materials

NEEDED: LOE whiteboard, Phonogram Cards b, n, d, Tactile Card b or b, *Doodling Dragons,* box or basket, scissors

OPTIONAL: Foods, books, and activities for "b" Day, Phonogram Game Tiles, squirt guns, chalkboard, finger paint and paper

Phonemic Awareness

Phonograms at the Beginning of Words

31.1 Sounds at the Beginning of Words

Read the phonogram in the corner. Say the sound. Circle all the pictures that start with that phonogram.

w - web, walrus, wagon
l - lizard, lion, lips, lamp
m - map, moon, mittens, mouse
n - nail, nest, necklace, net

Blends

Phonogram Cards
n, d

Show the Phonogram Card n.
What does this say? */n/*

Show the Phonogram Card d.
What does this say? */d/*

Hold them next to one another n d.
What do they say together? */nd/*

The Phonogram b

The Phonogram b

Show the Phonogram Card b.

This says /b/. What does it say? */b/*

Can you sing the sound /b/? *no*

Is part of your mouth blocking the sound? *yes, my lips*

Is /b/ a vowel or a consonant? *consonant*

Teacher Tip

Be sure to isolate the sound /b/. Be careful to not say /bŭ/.

b Day

Eat bananas, broccoli, bacon, bagels, beans, beets, bell peppers, biscuits, blackberries, blintzes, blueberries, or bread and butter. Ring bells. Learn about baboons, buffalo, bumblebees, badgers, bald eagles, bats, bears, or Bengal tigers. Play with balls, bats, blocks, or balloons, ride bikes, read books, make paper baskets. Wear blue, brown, and black. Dress up in bathrobes, baseball caps, or ballerina clothes. Look at the bark on trees. Go to the beach. Pour water from bottles into bowls.

Doodling Dragons: Sounds in Words

Doodling Dragons

Today we will read the /b/ page in *Doodling Dragons*.

Point to the phonogram b on the page.

What does this say? */b/*

Reread the page asking students to listen for /b/. Ask students to pretend to hit a ball with a bat when they hear the /b/ sound.

Handwriting

Writing the Phonogram b

Whiteboard
Phonogram Card b
Tactile Card b or b

Let's learn how to write /b/.

Demonstrate how to write /b/ using b or b.

Cursive Only: Show the Phonogram Card b and the Tactile Card b.

What do you notice is different? *The cursive /b/ loops to the top line, the circle is not closed, and there is a dip stroke.*

①**Loop** up to the top line, ②**down** to the baseline, ③**swing** up to the midline, ④**dip** connector at the midline. /b/

Start at the top line. ①**Straight** to the baseline, ②slide **up** to the midline, ③**circle** around to the baseline, ④touch. /b/

Write /b/ three times using your pointer finger.

Write /b/ three times on your whiteboard.
Which one sits on the baseline the best?
Which one goes up and touches the top line?
Which one looks most like the Tactile Card?
Put a smiley face next to the best /b/.

Writing on Paper

31.2 Handwriting Practice

Write /b/ three times on your favorite line size.
Circle your favorite /b/.

Phonogram Practice

The Phonogram Circuit

Set up 3-5 stations around the room with whiteboards, markers, and erasers. Tell students you will call out a phonogram sound. They need to run to each station, write it, then read it. When they get back to the starting point, call out a new sound.

Stations with whiteboards
Chalkboard
Squirt gun

Classroom: Phonogram Circuit

Divide the class into teams of 2-5 students. Set up 3-5 stations around the room with a whiteboard, marker and eraser for each team at each station. Each team should stand in a relay line. When you read the phonogram, the first student from each team runs to each of the stations, writes the phonogram, then runs back to start, and tags the next student who then runs the course writing the next phonogram.

Multi-Sensory Fun

Write phonograms on a waterproof whiteboard or chalkboard. Place the whiteboard outside, or in a bathtub or other waterproof area. Provide students with squirt guns. Read a phonogram's sound(s). Students may squirt the correct phonogram.

Words

Spelling List

Dictate the words for the students to write on their whiteboards or with Phonogram Game Tiles.

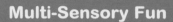

Multi-Sensory Fun

Write the words with finger paint.

Word	Sentence	Say to Spell	Markings	Spelling Hints
1. big	*The big truck honked.*	bĭg	big	All first sounds.
2. sand	*Let's build a castle in the sand.*	sănd	sand	All first sounds.
3. ran	*The dog ran away.*	răn	ran	All first sounds.
4. bad	*The cake tasted bad.*	băd	bad	All first sounds.
5. bend	*The wire will bend easily.*	bĕnd	bend	All first sounds.

Reading Practice

Reading Basketball

31.3 Reading Basketball

Cut out the words in your workbook.

Put them in a pile upside-down. Take one. Read it. Then crumple it up into a ball and try to shoot a basket.

Scissors

Basket or box

Teacher Tip

Each of the words has a blend using nd. Mastering this pattern is essential to developing fluency. This activity provides practice with the blend.

LESSON 32

Objectives

HANDWRITING: Learn the phonogram h.

PHONEMIC AWARENESS: Identify the beginning sound and match it to the phonogram. Practice blends.

WORDS: red, bat, hit, dot, band

Materials

NEEDED: LOE whiteboard, Phonogram Card h, Tactile Card h or h, Phonogram Game Cards, *Doodling Dragons*, scissors, glue, Reader 4

OPTIONAL: Foods, books, and activities for "h" Day, timer, Sandpaper Letters, Phonogram Game Tiles, chalkboard and chalk

Phonemic Awareness

Phonograms at the Beginning of Words

32.1 Sounds at the Beginning of Words

Look at the phonogram in the corner of the box. Say the sound. Circle all the pictures that start with the phonogram.

b - balloons, barn, bed, bear
r - rainbow, ring, rope, rake
s - sun, saw, sink, socks
t - turtle, tent, tree, turkey

The Phonogram h

The Phonogram h

Show the Phonogram Card h.

This says /h/. What does it say? ***/h/***

Can you sing the sound /h/? ***no***

Is /h/ a vowel or a consonant? ***consonant***

Phonogram Card h

h Day

Eat hamburgers, halibut, ham, hard rolls, hashbrowns, Hershey's Kisses, honeydew melon, hot chocolate, hot dogs, or hummus. Wear hats. Draw pictures of hands. Learn about hens, horses, hippos, hares, or hamsters. Honk horns. Build houses out of LEGO®s or Lincoln Logs. Learn to use a hammer. Play a harmonica. Make up secret handshakes.

Doodling Dragons: Sounds in Words

Today we will read the /h/ page in *Doodling Dragons*.

Point to the phonogram h on the page.

What does this say? ***/h/***

Reread the page asking students to listen for /h/. Ask students to clap their hands when they hear /h/.

Doodling Dragons

Challenge

Look at the "h" page. Segment a word from the picture aloud. Ask the student to point to the correct picture.

Handwriting

Writing the Phonogram h

Let's learn how to write /h/.

Demonstrate how to write /h/ using *h* or *h*.

Whiteboard
Phonogram Card h
Tactile Card *h* or *h*

Cursive Only: Show the Phonogram Card h and the Tactile Card *h*.

Compare how /h/ looks on the Phonogram Card to how it looks on the Tactile Card. What do you notice is different? ***The cursive /h/ starts with a loop instead of a straight line. There is a hook on the bottom of the cursive /h/.***

①**Loop** up to the top line,
②**straight** to the baseline,
③**bump** up to the midline,
④**down** to the baseline. /h/

Start at the top line. ①**Straight** to the baseline, ②**bump** up to the midline, ③**straight** to the baseline. /h/

Write /h/ three times using your pointer finger.

Write /h/ three times on your whiteboard.
Which one sits on the baseline the best?
Which one looks most like the Tactile Card?
Put a smiley face next to the best /h/.

Matching Bookface and Written Phonograms

32.2 Matching Phonograms

Match the bookface and handwritten phonograms.

Writing on Paper

32.3 Handwriting Practice

Write /h/ three times on your favorite line size.
Circle your favorite /h/.

Phonogram Practice

Run 'n' Match

Place a whiteboard at one end of the room and distribute the game cards for the phonograms learned thus far at the other end in a random pile. Say the sound(s) of a phonogram. The student writes it on the whiteboard, then checks to see if he is correct. If he wrote it correctly, he runs to the other end of the room, finds the matching game card, runs back to the whiteboard, holds it up, and reads the sound(s). Optional: Use a timer.

Phonogram Game Cards
Whiteboard
Timer
Sandpaper Letters

Multi-Sensory Fun

Use Sandpaper Letters.

Classroom: Run 'n' Match

Divide the class into teams of 3-4 students. Define a space for each team. Place a whiteboard at one end of the room and distribute one set of game cards for each team at the other end of the room. Tell students you will say the sound(s) of a phonogram. The first student on the team needs to write it on the whiteboard, check to see if he is correct, then run down to the other end of the room, find the matching game card, run back to the whiteboard, hold it up, and read the sound(s). When he finishes reading the sounds, the next student in line takes a turn.

Phonogram Game Cards
Whiteboard for each group

Challenge

Mix the cards for all the teams into a single pile.

Words

Spelling List

Dictate the words for the students to write on their whiteboards or with Phonogram Game Tiles.

Multi-Sensory Fun

Write words on a chalkboard.

	Word	Sentence	Say to Spell	Markings	Spelling Hints
1.	red	*The red car parked nearby.*	rĕd	red	All first sounds.
2.	bat	*He hit the ball with a bat.*	băt	bat	All first sounds.
3.	hit	*Hit the ball.*	hĭt	hit	All first sounds.
4.	dot	*There is a red dot on the page.*	dŏt	dot	All first sounds.
5.	band	*She plays a trumpet in the band.*	bănd	band	All first sounds.

Vocabulary

bat - Explore the various meanings. The bat and ball are in the garage. A bat flew in the night.

Reading Practice

Reader

Scissors
Glue

Reader 4

Read each page. Find the picture that matches. Glue it to the page. When you have finished, read the book aloud so that I can enjoy the illustrations.

LESSON 33

Objectives

HANDWRITING: Learn the phonogram k.

PHONEMIC AWARENESS: Create new words by changing the first sound. Practice blends.

WORDS: sink, honk, skunk, ink, link

Materials

NEEDED: LOE whiteboard, all the Phonogram Cards learned so far and k, Tactile Card k or k, Phonogram Game Tiles, *Doodling Dragons,* game pieces, scissors

OPTIONAL: Foods, books, and activities for "k" Day, rope for kangaroo tail

Phonemic Awareness

Creating New Words

Phonogram Game Tiles
a, b, c, d, h, l, m, p, r, s

Today we will make new words using Phonogram Game Tiles.

I have arranged the letters in a pattern. I want you to read the word I have created.

b	a	t

What does this say? ***bat***

If I take off the /b/ and replace it with a /h/, I can form a new word.

h	a	t

What does it say now? ***hat***

Teacher Tip

Do not require students to discover every possibility. Follow their natural interest.

Take off the /h/. What other letter could we place at the beginning to form a new word?

s	a	t

cat
pat
mat
rat

Let's try one more:

	a	d

What phonogram could you add to the beginning to form a new word?

dad *had* *pad*
sad *lad* *bad*
mad *tad*

The Phonogram k

The Phonogram k

Phonogram Card k

Show the Phonogram Card k.

This says /k/. What does it say? */k/*
Can you sing the sound /k/? *no*
Is /k/ a vowel or a consonant? *consonant*

k Day

Eat kale, ketchup, kiwi, and key lime pie. Learn about kangaroos, koalas, kangaroo rats, killer whales, and kittens. Fly kites. Kick a ball. Dress up like a king. Wear a kimono. Type on a keyboard. Play Keep-Away. Look through a kaleidoscope. Ride in a kayak. Play a kazoo. Learn how much a kilogram weighs.

Doodling Dragons: Sounds in Words

Doodling Dragons

Challenge

Look at the "k" page. Segment a word from the picture aloud. Ask the student to point to the correct picture.

Today we will read the /k/ page in *Doodling Dragons.*

Point to the phonogram k on the page.
What does this say? */k/*

Reread the page asking students to listen for /k/. Ask students to kick each time they hear the /k/ sound in a word.

Blends

Phonogram Cards
n, k

Show the Phonogram Card n.
What does this say? */n/*

Show the Phonogram Card k.
What does this say? */k/*

Hold them next to one another n k.
What do they say together? */nk/*

Handwriting

Writing the Kick Stroke

Whiteboard
Phonogram Card k
Tactile Card or
Tactile Card (manuscript kick) or
Rhythm of Handwriting Quick Reference

Today we will learn the kick stroke.

Show the Manuscript Tactile Card or use the Cursive Rhythm of Handwriting Quick Reference to teach the kick stroke. Demonstrate the stroke on the whiteboard as you explain the directions.

Start halfway between the midline and the baseline. **Kick.**

Practice writing the kick stroke three times on your whiteboard. Which one is the best? Why?

Writing the Phonogram k

Let's learn how to write /k/.

Demonstrate how to write /k/ using or .

Cursive Only: Show the Phonogram Card k and the Tactile Card .

What do you notice is different? ***The cursive /k/ loops to the top line. There is a curve at the midline rather than a straight line.***

①**Loop** up to the top line, ②**straight** to the baseline, ③slide **up** to the midline, ④**circle** around, ⑤touch halfway between the midline and the baseline, ⑥**kick** out to the baseline. /k/

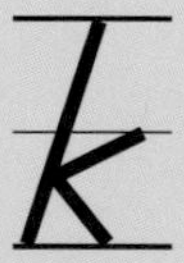

Start at the top line. ①**Straight** to the baseline, ②pick up your pencil, start at the midline, ③**slash** down to halfway between the midline and the baseline, ④touch, ⑤**kick** down to the baseline. /k/

Write /k/ three times using your pointer finger.

Write /k/ three times on your whiteboard.
Which one has the best kick?
Which one looks most like the Tactile Card?
Put a smiley face next to the best /k/.

Writing on Paper

33.1 Handwriting Practice

Write /k/ three times on your favorite line size.
Circle your favorite /k/.

Phonogram Practice

Phonogram Kangaroo

Ask the student to stand on one side of the room. Explain that you will show him a card. If he reads it correctly, he can take one kangaroo hop forward. If he does not read it correctly, he needs to go back to the beginning. When he reaches the other side of the room, he wins.

Phonogram Cards
a, b, c, d, e, g, h, i, j, k l, m, n, o, p, qu, r, s, t, u, w
rope to create a kangaroo tail

Words

Spelling List

Dictate the words for the students to write on their whiteboards or with Phonogram Game Tiles. See the sample script on the next page.

Teacher Tip

Tell students to use "tall k" rather than /k-s/. Dictation is a method to teach new words, not to test prior knowledge.

Word	Sentence	Say to Spell	Markings	Spelling Hints
1. sink	*Wash your hands in the sink.*	sĭnk	sink	All first sounds.
2. honk	*Cars on the street honk.*	hŏnk	honk	All first sounds.
3. skunk	*The skunk smells bad.*	skŭnk	skunk	All first sounds.
4. ink	*The ink on the card smeared.*	ĭnk	ink	All first sounds.
5. link	*Link the pieces together.*	lĭnk	link	All first sounds.

sink

The first word is *sink*. Wash your hands in the sink. *sink*

Now it is your turn to say "sink." Then sound it out.
sink /s-ĭ-n-k/.

Use a tall /k/.

Write the word on your whiteboard. As you write it, say each of the sounds aloud. */s-ĭ-n-k/*

Multi-Sensory Fun

If students struggle with the blend NK, show the n and k phonogram cards. Practice reading the sounds individually, then as blends, then separating the blend into two sounds.

The student writes *sink* on his whiteboard.

It is now my turn to write *sink*. I want you to drive my marker by sounding it out. */s-ĭ-n-k/*

The student sounds out */s-ĭ-n-k/* while the teacher writes the word on the board.

Let's read it together. Point to each phonogram as you read it. Then blend the word together.
/s-ĭ-n-k/ sink

Vocabulary

Sink - Explore the multiple meanings of sink by asking students to use it in sentences. The sink is full of water. The stones sink quickly. That is a sink hole. I have a sinking feeling about it.

Reading Practice

Matching Game

33.2 Matching Game

Read the word or phrase. Draw a line to the picture that matches it.

Blending Practice

Game pieces
Scissors

33.3 Blending Game

Cut out the game cards. Place them face down in three piles sorted by color. Place a game piece on the board. The student draws a card that matches the color space her game piece is on. When she reaches red, she may choose any color card to read. Each time she reads it correctly without help, she may advance two spaces. Each time she reads it correctly with help, she may advance one space.

Teacher Tip

Save the game board and cards to reuse in the next lesson.

LESSON 34

Objectives

HANDWRITING: Learn the phonogram f.

PHONEMIC AWARENESS: Create new words by changing the first sound.

WORDS: fast, nest, list, best, last

Materials

NEEDED: LOE whiteboard, Phonogram Cards f, s, t, Tactile Card f or f, Phonogram Game Tiles, *Doodling Dragons*, scissors, game pieces

OPTIONAL: Foods, books, and activities for "f" Day, mirror, window paint

Phonemic Awareness

Creating New Words

Phonogram Game Tiles
a, b, c, d, e, g, h, i, j, k, l, m, n, o, p, qu, r, s, t, u, w

Today we will make new words using Phonogram Game Tiles. Read the word I have created.

b	i	t

What does this say? *bit*

If I take off the /b/ and replace it with a /h/, I can form a new word.

h	i	t

What does this say? *hit*

Take off the /h/. What letter could we place there to form a new word?

s	i	t

quit	*lit*
pit	*kit*

Let's try one more:

	e	t

What phonogram could you add to the beginning to form a new word? ***answers will vary***

pet	*jet*	*met*
get	*wet*	*let*
set	*net*	*bet*

Blends

Phonogram Cards

s, t

Show the Phonogram Card s.

What does this say? */s/*

Show the Phonogram Card t.

What does this say? */t/*

Hold them next to one another s t.

What do they say together? */st/*

The Phonogram f

The Phonogram f

Phonogram Card f

Show the Phonogram Card f

This says /f/. What does it say? */f/*

Can you sing the sound /f/? ***no***

Is /f/ a vowel or a consonant? ***consonant***

f Day

Eat fish, french fries, fajitas, flat bread, feta cheese, fettuccine, figs, or fudge. Learn about frogs, fireflies, flamingos, or foxes. Learn how to floss. Make fairies or paper flowers. Visit a fire station or a farm. Buy fish. Make a flag. Take a walk in the forest.

Doodling Dragons: Sounds in Words

Doodling Dragons

Today we will read the /f/ page in *Doodling Dragons*.

Point to the phonogram f on the page.

What does this say? */f/*

Reread the page asking students to listen for /f/. Ask students to flap their arms each time they hear the /f/ sound.

Challenge

Look at the "f" page. Segment a word from the picture aloud. Ask the student to point to the correct picture.

Handwriting

Writing the Phonogram f

Let's learn how to write /f/.

Demonstrate how to write /f/ using *f* or f.

Whiteboard
Phonogram Card f
Tactile Card *f* or f

Cursive Only: Show the Phonogram Card f and the Tactile Card *f*.

What do you notice is different? *The cursive /f/ loops to the top line and it drops below the baseline. The bookface /f/ has a cross at the midline.*

Draw a cursive /f/ on the board. Then write a manuscript /f/ over the top in a different color. lining them up so the cross is on the baseline.

Though the ways we write the cursive /f/ and the bookface /f/ are different, when we write them like this we can see the relationship between their shapes.

①**Loop** up to the top line, ②**drop** down halfway below the baseline, ③**hook** up to the baseline, ④touch at the baseline, ⑤**glide**. /f/

Start just below the top line.
①**Roll** around past the top line, ②**straight** to the baseline, ③pick up the pencil, ④**cross** at the midline. /f/

Write /f/ three times using your pointer finger.

Write /f/ three times on your whiteboard.
Which one looks most like the Tactile Card?
Put a smiley face next to the best /f/.

Writing on Paper

34.1 Handwriting Practice

Write /f/ three times on your favorite line size.
Circle your favorite /f/.

Phonogram Practice

Blind Writing

Call out a phonogram by sound(s). Ask the students to write it on their whiteboard with their eyes closed. Practice the phonograms that students have not yet mastered.

Whiteboard

Words

Spelling List

Dictate the words for the students to write on their whiteboards or with Phonogram Game Tiles.

Multi-Sensory Fun

Write the words on a mirror or window with window paint.

Word	Sentence	Say to Spell	Markings	Spelling Hints
1. fast	*The girl ran fast.*	făst	fast	All first sounds.
1. nest	*The bird built a nest in the tree.*	nĕst	nest	All first sounds.
2. list	*Make a list of supplies.*	lĭst	list	All first sounds.
3. best	*This is the best soup!*	bĕst	best	All first sounds.
4. last	*This is his last chance.*	lăst	last	All first sounds.

Reading Practice

Blending Practice 2

34.2 Blending Game

Scissors
Game pieces
Game board and cards from Lesson 33

Cut out the game cards and mix them with the cards from Lesson 33. Place them face down in four piles sorted by color. Place a game piece on the game board from Lesson 33. The student draws a card that matches the color space her game piece is on. Each time she reads it correctly without help, she may advance two spaces. Each time she reads it correctly with help, she may advance one space.

LESSON 35

Objectives

HANDWRITING: Learn the phonogram v.

PHONEMIC AWARENESS: Blend multi-syllable words.

WORDS: van, vest, kid, win, rest

Materials

NEEDED: LOE whiteboard, Phonogram Card v, Tactile Card v or v, *Doodling Dragons*, two sets of Phonogram Game Cards, hat or basket, scissors, glue, Reader 5

OPTIONAL: Foods, books, and activities for "v" Day, Phonogram Game Tiles

Phonemic Awareness

Blending Multi-Syllable Words

35.1 Multi-Syllable Words

Today I will segment a word. I want you to blend it back together, shout out the name of the animal, and point to it.

/ē-g-l/	eagle
/p-ă-n-d-ä/	panda
/k-ĭ-t-ĕ-n/	kitten
/j-er-ă-f/	giraffe
/t-er-k-ē/	turkey
/z-ē-b-r-ä/	zebra
/s-qu-er-ĕ-l/	squirrel
/l-ī-ŏ-n/	lion

Challenge

Segment the name of an animal and ask the child to blend it without the visual reference of the worksheet.

Multi-Sensory Fun

Once he blends the word, ask the child to act like the animal.

The Phonogram v

The Phonogram v

Show the Phonogram Card v.

This says /v/. What does it say? ***/v/***

Can you sing the sound /v/? ***no***

Is /v/ a vowel or a consonant? ***consonant***

Doodling Dragons: Sounds in Words

Today we will read the /v/ page in *Doodling Dragons.*

Point to the phonogram v on the page.

What does this say? ***/v/***

Reread the page asking students to listen for /v/. Ask students to swerve each time they hear the /v/ sound in a word.

Phonogram Card v
Doodling Dragons

v Day

Eat vegetables. Make vegetable soup. Mix vinegar and baking soda to see the reaction. Listen to violin music. Learn about voles or vultures. Put flowers in a vase. Draw a picture of a van. Vroom toy vehicles.

Handwriting

Writing the Phonogram v

Let's learn how to write /v/.

Demonstrate how to write /v/ using v or v.

Whiteboard
Phonogram Card v
Tactile Card v or v
Rhythm of Handwriting Quick Reference

Cursive Only: Show the Phonogram Card v and the Tactile Card v.

Compare how /v/ looks on the Phonogram Card to how it looks in your workbook. What do you notice is different? ***It curves up before it goes down. It has a dip connector.***

Manuscript Only: Teach the angle up stroke using the Rhythm of Handwriting Manuscript Quick Reference. Demonstrate the stroke on the whiteboard as you explain the directions.

First, we will learn the angle up stroke. *Start at the baseline.* **Angle up** to the midline.

Practice writing the angle up stroke three times on your whiteboard. Which one is the best? Why?

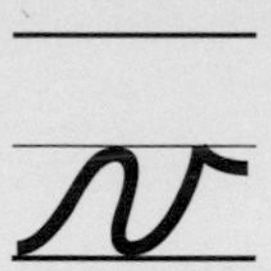

①**Bump** up to the midline, ②**down** to the baseline, ③**swing** up to the midline, ④**dip** connector at the midline. /v/

Start at the midline. ①**Kick** down to the baseline, ②**angle up** to the midline. /v/

Write /v/ three times using your pointer finger.

Write /v/ three times on your whiteboard.
Which one sits on the baseline the best?
Which one is touching the midline but does not go over the midline?
Which one looks most like the Tactile Card?
Put a smiley face next to the best /v/.

Matching Bookface and Written Phonograms

35.2 Matching Phonograms

Match the bookface and handwritten phonograms.

Writing on Paper

35.3 Handwriting Practice

Write /v/ three times on your favorite line size.
Circle your favorite /v/.

Phonogram Practice

Go Fish

2 sets of Phonogram Game Cards per group of 4 students
a, b, c, d, e, f, g, h, i, j, k, l, m, n, o, p, qu, r, s, t, u, w

1) Mix two sets of Phonogram Game Cards together. 2) Deal seven cards to each player. Place the remaining cards in the middle of the table face down and spread them out into a "fishing pond." 3) Player A chooses a player (Player B) to ask, "Do you have a __?" Player A should ask for a match to a phonogram he has in his hand, naming the phonogram by its sound(s). 4) If the answer is "yes," Player B must give the requested card to him, and Player A lays the matched cards down in front of him and takes another turn. 5) If the answer is "no," Player B should say, "Go fish." Player A then draws a card from the pond. If a match is found, it is laid down and Player A repeats his turn. If no match is found, play moves to the next player on the left. 6) Play until all the cards have been matched. The player with the most matches wins.

Words

Spelling List

Dictate the words for the students to write on their whiteboards or with Phonogram Game Tiles.

Word	Sentence	Say to Spell	Markings	Spelling Hints
1. van	*A red van stopped at the corner.*	văn	van	All first sounds.
2. vest	*I wore a warm vest.*	věst	vest	All first sounds.
3. kid	*The kid ran across the park.*	kĭd	kid	All first sounds.
4. win	*Did he win the race?*	wĭn	win	All first sounds.
5. rest	*It is time to rest.*	rěst	rest	All first sounds.

Reading Practice

Charades

35.4 Charades

Scissors
Hat or basket

Cut out the words and fold them in half. Ask the student to draw a word, read it silently to himself, then act it out. You (and the other students) should guess what he is acting out.

vest	bat	mom
frog	bag	sink
cat	sand	fan
dog	mad	hot
skunk	sad	pig
milk	dad	gum

Reader

Reader 5

Scissors
Glue

Read the page. Find the picture that matches. Glue the picture to the page. When you have finished, read the book aloud to me.

REVIEW LESSON G

Area	Skill	Mastery
Phonemic Awareness	Independently identify the initial sound of a word.	1
	Blend nd, nk, st.	2
	Create new words by changing the initial sound.	2
	Blend multi-syllable words.	3
Handwriting	Write n, m, e, l.	1
	Write b, h, k, f, v.	2
Phonograms	Read n, m, e, l.	1
	Read b, h, k, f, v.	2
Reading	Read CVC words.	2
	Read one-syllable words with consonant blends.	2

Phonemic Awareness Assessment

Beginning Phonograms

G.1 Phonemic Awareness

Read the phonogram. Circle all the pictures which start with that sound.

k - king, kitten, kite

b - ball, barn, baby, bird

Read the word. Which other letters from the letter bank can you substitute to make a new word? Write it in the blank or circle it.

Handwriting Assessment

Handwriting

G.2 Handwriting

Choose the line size that you prefer. Write one of each phonogram.

Multi-Sensory Fun

If the student is not ready to write on paper, show the student the Phonogram Card and have him write the phonogram on a whiteboard or in a sensory box.

Phonogram Assessment

What's That Phonogram?

G.3 What's That Phonogram?

On your page are groups of four phonograms. I will say a phonogram's sound(s). Color the phonogram with your highlighter.

1. /b/
2. /l/
3. /n/
4. /m/
5. /ĕ-ē/
6. /f/
7. /v/
8. /h/
9. /k/

Highlighter

Challenge

The ideal handwriting and phonogram assessment would be to dictate the phonogram sound(s) for the student to write on a whiteboard or on paper without a visual reference. These phonograms may be considered mastered.

Phonogram Assessment

Ask the student to read each of the following Phonogram Cards: n, m, e, l, b, h, k, f, v

Phonogram Cards
n, m, e, l, b, h, k, f, v

Reading Assessment

Reading

G.4 Reading

Read the word. Match it to the picture.

Teacher Tip

The first page includes only CVC words. The second page includes blends. Listen to the student read samples from both pages.

Practice Ideas

Sounds at The Beginning of Words

Set out a group of objects such as stuffed animals. Choose a phonogram card. Ask the student to place all the objects that begin with the targeted phonogram next to the card.

Give the student a phonogram card. Ask him to run around the room finding things in the room that begin with the targeted sound. He should hold up the card, say the sound, then say the object's name.

Handwriting

Reteach how to write any of the phonograms that are difficult for the students using the Tactile Cards. Break down each step and have the student repeat the short, bold directions aloud.

"Phonogram Journey" on page 121
"Blind Writing" on page 137
"Word Quilt" on page 157
"The Phonogram Circuit" on page 163
"Run 'n' Match" on page 167

Teacher Tip

Students who struggle with handwriting should practice writing using large motor movements. It is also beneficial for these students to recite the bold, rhythmic directions aloud when writing.

Phonograms

- “Slap It!” on page 118
- “Rotten Egg” on page 128
- “Snatch the Phonogram” on page 151
- "Phonogram Kangaroo" on page 173
- "Go Fish" on page 181

Reading Words

- “Act it Out” on page 114
- “Read and Do” on page 143
- "Reading Basketball" on page 164
- "Charades" on page 182

Reading Blends

- "Blending Practice" on page 174
- "Blending Practice 2" on page 178

Teacher Tip

If the student is still uncertain about reading CVC words, practice with games that use only this form first. Then move ahead to practicing words with consonant blends. Many students at this stage will still find blending two or more consonants difficult. If the student demonstrates understanding of the concept, continue with Lessons 36-40. Additional practice will be provided.

Teacher Tip

Reading at this stage will still not be fluent. The student should continue to Lessons 36-40 if he is attempting to sound out words, is reading 50% or more of the words in the lessons correctly on his own, and shows a desire to move ahead. Fluency varies greatly among students at this stage.

LESSON 36

Objectives

HANDWRITING: Learn the phonogram x.

PHONEMIC AWARENESS: Learn about short vowel sounds and how to mark them.

WORDS: box, milk, tent, wax, fist

Materials

NEEDED: LOE whiteboard, all the Phonogram Cards learned so far and x, Tactile Cards z or z (slash) and x or x, *Doodling Dragons,* bell or buzzer, scissors

OPTIONAL: Foods, books, and activities for "x" Day, Phonogram Game Tiles, obstacles

Phonemic Awareness

Review Vowels and Consonants

I will show you a phonogram. Tell me if it is a vowel or a consonant. Then tell me why.

Phonogram Cards
a, b, e, i, j, m, o, u

Show the Phonogram Card a.
vowel I can sing all the sounds. My mouth is open.

Show the Phonogram Card e.
vowel I can sing all the sounds. My mouth is open.

Show the Phonogram Card b.
consonant I cannot sing /b/. My lips are blocking the sound.

Show the Phonogram Card m.
consonant My mouth is closed. My lips are blocking the sound.

Show the Phonogram Card j.
consonant I cannot sing /j/. My tongue is blocking the sound.

Short Vowels

Have you ever noticed that all the vowels make more than one sound?
Each of the vowel sounds has a name. Today we will learn the name of the first vowel sound.
The first vowel sound is called the short sound.
Let's read the vowels but read only the short sounds.

Show the Phonogram Card a.
/ă/

Show the Phonogram Card e.
/ĕ/

Show the Phonogram Card i.
/ĭ/

Show the Phonogram Card o.
/ŏ/

Show the Phonogram Card u.
/ŭ/

Now I will show you how to mark the short vowel sound. We write a curved line over it. This is called a breve.

Write ă.
/ă/

Write ĕ.
/ĕ/

Write ĭ.
/ĭ/

Write ŏ.
/ŏ/

Write ŭ.
/ŭ/

Vocabulary

Breve means short. This root is also found in words such as: abbreviate (to shorten), abbreviation (a shortened form), and brevity (a short time).

Let's read the short vowel sounds. While we read them, put your hands over our head in a curved shape.

Point to the short vowels on the board as you read them aloud.

The Phonogram x

The Phonogram x

Show the Phonogram Card x.

This says /ks-z/. What does it say? */ks-z/*

Can you sing the sound /ks/? *no*

Is something blocking the sound? *Yes, my tongue is blocking the sound.*

Is /ks/ a vowel or a consonant? *consonant*

Can you sing the sound /z/? *no*

Is something blocking the sound? *Yes, my tongue is blocking the sound.*

Is /z/ a vowel or a consonant? *consonant*

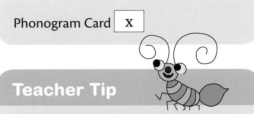

Phonogram Card x

Teacher Tip

/z/ is not a common sound made the by the X phonogram. Therefore, in *LOE Essentials,* the /z/ sound is taught as an advanced phonogram sound. However, /z/ is commonly associated with xylophone in ABC books and thus is included in *Doodling Dragons* and *Foundations.*

x Day

Learn about ibexes, foxes and oxen. Play with boxes. Learn how to fix something. Learn to write the number six. Mix cookie dough. Make wax candles.

Doodling Dragons: Sounds in Words

Today we will read the /ks-z/ page in *Doodling Dragons.*

Doodling Dragons

Point to the phonogram x on the page.

What does this say? */ks-z/*

Reread the page asking students to listen for /ks/. Ask students to put their arms in the shape of an X each time they hear the /ks/ sound in a word. Repeat for the /z/ sound.

Handwriting

Writing the Slash Stroke

Today we will learn the slash stroke.

Show the Tactile Card  or . Demonstrate the stroke on the card as you explain the directions.

Practice writing the slash stroke three times on your whiteboard. Which one is the best? Why?

Whiteboard
Phonogram Card x
Tactile Card  or  (slash)
Tactile Card 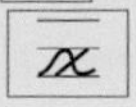 or 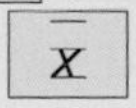

Writing the Phonogram x

Let's learn how to write /ks/.

Demonstrate how to write /ks/ using x or x.

Cursive Only: Show the Phonogram Card x and the Tactile Card x.

Compare how we write /ks/ to how it appears in books. What do you notice is different? *The cursive /ks/ bumps up to the midline, the stroke is not straight at the bottom.*

①**Bump** up to the midline, ②**kick** down to the baseline, ③pick up the pencil, start at the midline, ④**slash** down to the baseline. /ks/

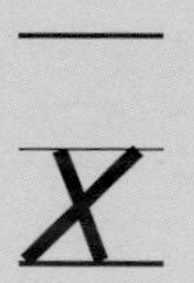

Start at the midline. ①**Kick** down to the baseline, ②pick up the pencil, start at the midline, ③**slash** down to the baseline. /ks/

Write /ks/ three times using your pointer finger.

Write /ks/ three times on your whiteboard.
Which one is touching the baseline but not going under it?
Which one is touching the midline but not going over it?
Which one looks most like the Tactile Card?
Put a smiley face next to the best /ks/.

Writing on Paper

36.1 Handwriting Practice

Write /ks/ three times on your favorite line size.
Circle the best /ks/.

Phonogram Practice

Teacher Trouble

Explain that today you have forgotten your phonograms and you need the student(s) to drill you. Students must show you a Phonogram Card and you will say the sound(s). When you make a mistake the student(s) will ring the bell or say, "buzz." Be sure to get plenty wrong!

Bell or buzzer
Phonogram Cards
a, b, c, d, e, f, g, h, i, j, k, l, m, n, o, p, qu, r, s, t, u, w, x

Words

Spelling List

Dictate the words for the students to write on their whiteboards or with Phonogram Game Tiles.

Word	Sentence	Say to Spell	Markings	Spelling Hints
1. box	*The shoes are in the box.*	bŏks	box	All first sounds.
2. milk	*Drink your milk.*	mĭlk	milk	All first sounds.
3. tent	*We will stay in a tent.*	tĕnt	tent	All first sounds.
4. wax	*The candle is made of wax.*	wăks	wax	All first sounds.
5. fist	*He clenched his fist.*	fĭst	fist	All first sounds.

Reading Practice

Matching

36.2 Matching

Draw a line from each word to the matching picture.

High Frequency Word Run

36.3 High Frequency Words

Cut out the words. Designate a place for words that are unread, and place them upside down in a pile. Designate a place across the room for words that have been read. The student chooses a word, reads it aloud, then runs it to the other side of the room.

High Frequency Word Run: Classroom

Play the same game above; however, divide the class into teams and provide a stack of words for each team.

Teacher Tip

Save the high frequency words for use in later lessons. 300 high frequency words comprise approximately 50% of all that we read and write in English. Mastering these words is essential to reading fluency and comprehension.

Scissors

Obstacles

Multi-Sensory Fun

Place obstacles between the two piles of cards for the student to run around, jump over, crawl under...

LESSON 37

Objectives

HANDWRITING: Learn the phonogram y.

PHONEMIC AWARENESS: Review the short vowel sounds.

WORDS: yes, jump, six, skin, skip

Materials

NEEDED: LOE whiteboard, Phonogram Card y, Tactile Card y or y, *Doodling Dragons*, two sets of Phonogram Game Cards, scissors

OPTIONAL: Foods, books, and activities for "y" Day, Phonogram Game Tiles

Phonemic Awareness

Short Vowels

Write ă.

In the last lesson we learned something new. What does breve mean?

It is a short vowel. It says its first sound. It says /ă/.

Let's read the short vowel sounds as I write them on the board.

Write ĕ.

/ĕ/

Write ĭ.

/ĭ/

Write ŏ.

/ŏ/

Write ŭ.

/ŭ/

37.1 Short Vowel Sounds

In your workbook you have five vowels. I will read a sound. Circle the correct sound.

/ŭ/ /ă/
/ĭ/ /ŏ/
/ĕ/

Challenge

Read a short vowel sound. Ask the student to write the vowel including the breve.

The Phonogram y

The Phonogram y

Show the Phonogram Card y.

This says /y-ĭ-ī-ē/. What does it say? ***/y-ĭ-ī-ē/***
How many sounds is this? ***four***

Can you sing the first sound /y/? ***no***
Is /y/ a vowel or a consonant sound? ***consonant***

Can you sing the second sound /ĭ/ and is your mouth open? ***yes***
Is /ĭ/ a vowel or a consonant sound? ***vowel***

Can you sing the third sound /ī/ and is your mouth open? ***yes***
Is /ī/ a vowel or a consonant sound? ***vowel***

Can you sing the fourth sound /ē/ and is your mouth open? ***yes***
Is /ē/ a vowel or a consonant sound? ***vowel***

That is interesting. /y-ĭ-ī-ē/ is both a vowel and a consonant.

y Day

Wear yellow. Read about yaks and yachts. Eat yams, yogurt, and egg yolks. Play in the yard. Learn to measure with a yardstick.

Doodling Dragons: Sounds in Words

Today we will read the /y-ĭ-ī-ē/ page in *Doodling Dragons*.

Point to the phonogram y on the page.

What does this say? */y-ĭ-ī-ē/*

Reread the page asking students to listen for each of the sounds.

Doodling Dragons

Handwriting

Writing the Phonogram y

Whiteboard
Phonogram Card y
Tactile Card y or y

Let's learn how to write /y-ĭ-ī-ē/.

Demonstrate how to write /y-ĭ-ī-ē/ using y or y.

Cursive Only: Show the Phonogram Card y and the Tactile Card y.

Compare how we write /y-ĭ-ī-ē/ to how it appears in books. *The cursive begins with a bump to the midline. Also the swoop touches the baseline.*

①**Bump** up to the midline, ②**down** to the baseline, ③**swing** up to the midline, ④**drop** down halfway below the baseline, ⑤**swoop**. /y-ĭ-ī-ē/

Start at the midline. ①**Down** to the baseline, ②**swing** up to the midline, ③**drop** down half-way below the baseline, ④small **swoop**. /y-ĭ-ī-ē/

Write /y-ĭ-ī-ē/ three times using your pointer finger.

Write /y-ĭ-ī-ē/ three times on your whiteboard.
Which one looks most like the Tactile Card?
Put a smiley face next to the best /y-ĭ-ī-ē/.

Writing on Paper

37.2 Handwriting Practice

Write /y-ĭ-ī-ē/ three times on your favorite line size.
Which /y-ĭ-ī-ē/ is the neatest?

Phonogram Practice

Phonogram Snatch

2 sets of Phonogram Game Cards

1) Lay out eight to sixteen game cards face up. 2) Read the sound(s) for one of the phonograms. 3) The student should snatch the matching card(s) as quickly as possible. 4) Replace the cards as they are removed.

Classroom: Phonogram Snatch

In a classroom, play Phonogram Snatch with groups of 2-6 students. One student will read the sound(s) and the others will race to snatch the matching card.

2 sets of Phonogram Game Cards for each group of 2-6 students

Words

Spelling List

Dictate the words for the students to write on their whiteboards or with Phonogram Game Tiles.

Word	Sentence	Say to Spell	Markings	Spelling Hints
1. yes	*Yes, we will go soon.*	yĕs	yes	All first sounds.
2. jump	*Watch the cat jump.*	jŭmp	jump	All first sounds.
3. six	*She is six years old.*	sĭks	six	All first sounds.
4. skin	*Put sunscreen on your skin.*	skĭn	skin	All first sounds.
5. skip	*I like to skip stones on the water.*	skĭp	skip	All first sounds.

Reading Practice

Reading Practice

Scissors

37.3 Phrases

Cut out the words. Ask students to read the words and arrange them into phrases, such as: red fox, big cat, tan box.

Read and Move Blending Practice

Write a word on the board. Ask students to read the word and do the action.

swim
step
stop
stink
spin
rest
jump
limp
bend
stand
trot

sit
dig
sip
pat
run
hum
jog
nap
tap

Teacher Tip

Each of the words in the first column includes a blend. Offer a lot of support by modeling how to sound out the words if needed.

Teacher Tip

If the student becomes frustrated with blends, mix in some of the words in the second column.

LESSON 38

Objectives

HANDWRITING: Learn the phonogram [z].

PHONEMIC AWARENESS: Learn about long vowel sounds.

WORDS: if, zip, fox, flag, flap

Materials

NEEDED: LOE whiteboard, Phonogram Cards [a], [e], [i], [o], [u], [z], Tactile Card [z] or [z], *Doodling Dragons,* game pieces, die, scissors

OPTIONAL: Foods, books, and activities for "z" Day, Phonogram Game Tiles

Phonemic Awareness

Long Vowels

Phonogram Cards
a, e, i, o, u

In the last lessons we learned about short vowels. What is a short vowel? *the first vowel sound*

How do we mark it? *put a curved line over it*

Today we will learn about the second sound of each vowel. This is called the long sound. Let's try to read the phonograms, but only say the second sound out loud.

Show the Phonogram Card [a].

/ā/

Show the Phonogram Card [e].

/ē/

Show the Phonogram Card i.

/ī/

Show the Phonogram Card o.

/ō/

Show the Phonogram Card u.

/ū/

Did you know you just read the names for each of these phonograms? All the single-letter phonograms also have a name. For the vowels, the name is the same as the long sound. Now I will show you how to mark the long vowel sound. We write a straight line over it.

I will write the long vowels on the board. Read each sound.

Write ā.

/ā/

Write ē.

/ē/

Write ī.

/ī/

Write ō.

/ō/

Write ū.

/ū/

Teacher Tip

We will introduce the multiple long /ū/ sounds in Level B.

Teacher Tip

U has two long /ū/ sounds, /ū/ and /oo/. These can be heard by comparing words such as *cute* and *flute*. When we compare the sounds made in these words, we discover that /ū/ and /oo/ are very similar. The only difference is the initial sound /y/ is dropped. The fourth sound of U, /ü/, is the broad sound found in words such as *butcher, pudding,* and *put*.

Short and Long Vowels

I will say a vowel sound. If it is a long sound I want you to stretch your arms into a long line and say, "long." If it is a short sound I want you to curve your arms and say, "short."

ŭ	ă	ŏ
ō	ē	ū
ā	ī	

38.1 Long and Short Vowel Sounds

In your workbook you will see vowels. I will read a sound. Circle the correct sound.

ē	ĭ	ă
ū	ā	

The Phonogram z

The Phonogram z

Show the Phonogram Card z.

This says /z/. What does it say? */z/*
Can you sing the sound /z/? *no*

Is /z/ a vowel or a consonant? *consonant*

Phonogram Card z

z Day

Eat zucchini and zwieback toast. Go to the zoo. Learn about zebras and zebra fish. Discover different types of zippers. Draw zig-zag lines.

Doodling Dragons: Sounds in Words

Today we will read the /z/ page in *Doodling Dragons.*

Point to the phonogram z on the page.

What does this say? */z/*

Reread the page asking students to listen for /z/. Ask students to pretend they are asleep each time they hear the /z/ sound.

Doodling Dragons

Handwriting

Writing The Phonogram z

Let's learn how to write /z/.

Demonstrate how to write /z/ using z or z.

Whiteboard
Phonogram Card z
Tactile Card z or z

Cursive Only: Show the Phonogram Card z and the Tactile Card z.

Compare the two forms of /z/. *They look very different. The cursive /z/ bumps up to the midline. It also swoops below the baseline. The bookface /z/ has straight lines. It sits between the baseline and the midline.*

①**Bump** up to the midline, ②**tuck** down to the baseline, ③**drop** down halfway below the baseline, ④**swoop**. /z/

Start at the midline. ①**Cross** at the midline, ②**slash** down to the baseline, ③**cross** at the baseline. /z/

Write /z/ three times using your pointer finger.
Write /z/ three times on your whiteboard.
Which one looks most like the Tactile Card?
Put a smiley face next to the best /z/.

Teacher Tip

Z is not commonly used in English. The most common spelling of the /z/ sound is S. However, S never spells the sound /z/ at the beginning of the word. The sound /z/ at the beginning is always spelled with a Z.

Writing on Paper

38.2 Handwriting Practice

Write /z/ three times on your favorite line size.
Circle your favorite /z/.

Phonogram Practice

Phonogram Board Game

38.3 Phonogram Board Game

1) The student rolls the die and advances the number of spaces shown on the die. 2) He must read each of the phonograms as he passes. 3) If the phonograms are read correctly, the student may stay at that spot. 4) If a phonogram is not read correctly, the student must return to the original space.

Words

Spelling List

Dictate the words for the students to write on their whiteboards or with Phonogram Game Tiles.

Word	Sentence	Say to Spell	Markings	Spelling Hints
1. if	*If it is hot, we will go to the pool.*	ĭf	if	All first sounds.
2. zip	*Zip your coat.*	zĭp	zip	All first sounds.
3. fox	*The fox trotted around the pen.*	fŏks	fox	All first sounds.
4. flag	*That is the American flag.*	flăg	flag	All first sounds.
5. flap	*The flag flaps in the wind.*	flăp	flap	All first sounds.

Reading Practice

High Frequency Word Maze

38.4 High Frequency Words

Lay out the words in a maze that winds through the room. As the student reads each word, he may step on it and advance through the maze. In a classroom, set up multiple mazes and divide the class into teams.

Scissors

Teacher Tip

Save the high frequency word cards to be used in future games. Combine them with the cards from Lesson 36.

LESSON 39

Objectives

PHONEMIC AWARENESS: Review short and long vowel sounds.

WORDS: bed, sun, wind, stomp, stamp

Materials

NEEDED: LOE whiteboard, Phonogram Cards, small crackers or chocolate chips for Bingo, obstacles for the obstacle course, scissors, glue, Reader 6

OPTIONAL: Phonogram Game Tiles, clipboards, blank paper

Phonemic Awareness

Short and Long Vowel Sounds

39.1 Short and Long Vowel Sounds

Read each of the vowels in your workbook aloud. Do you remember what the markings mean? ***The breve means it is a short sound. The line means the vowel is saying its long sound or its name.***

Vowels

I will show you a phonogram. Then I will say a vowel sound. If it is a long sound, stretch your arms into a long line and say, "long." If it is a short sound, curve your arms and say, "short."

ă	ī	ē
ō	ū	ŏ
ŭ	ā	

Phonogram Practice

Phonogram Bingo

39.2 Phonogram Bingo

Small crackers or chocolate chips for Bingo

Read a phonogram's sound(s). The student covers it. When the whole Bingo card has been covered, the student should read the sound(s) back. He may then eat the treat.

Phonogram Obstacle Course

Whiteboard
or blank paper and clipboard
Phonogram Cards
Obstacles for the obstacle course

Set up nine stations around the room. At each station place a phonogram card and marker. Between each of the stations place an obstacle to run around, a table to crawl under, something to balance on, or something to climb over. Demonstrate to the students how to go through the obstacle course. Provide each student with a whiteboard or a clipboard with paper. When they see a phonogram, they need to stop, read it, write it on the whiteboard while saying the short directions aloud, and show it to you. When you nod "yes," they can go on to the next obstacle.

Classroom: Obstacle Course

Assign a student referee to each phonogram station. The referee needs to make sure the phonogram is read and written correctly. When one student finishes the course, he then moves into the position of referee for the first station and all the referees move forward one station. This will free one referee to move into the line to complete the obstacle course.

Teacher Tip

Students who act as referees gain a lot of repeated exposure to the phonogram at their station. This is a great way to help students who are struggling with a phonogram to gain additional practice and confidence.

Words

Spelling List

Dictate the words for the students to write on their whiteboards or with Phonogram Game Tiles.

Word	Sentence	Say to Spell	Markings	Spelling Hints
1. bed	*It is time to go to bed.*	bĕd	bed	All first sounds.
2. sun	*The sun is shining brightly.*	sŭn	sun	All first sounds.
3. wind	*The wind is blowing.*	wĭnd	wind	All first sounds.
4. stomp	*We will stomp around the room.*	stŏmp	stomp	All first sounds.
5. stamp	*Put a stamp on the letter.*	stămp	stamp	All first sounds.

Reading Practice

Reader

Scissors
Glue

Reader 6

Read the page. Find the picture that matches. Glue it in.

When you have finished, read the book aloud to me.

LESSON 40

Objectives

PHONOGRAMS: Celebrate the students' progress in learning A-Z.

Materials

NEEDED: Many optional activities are included. Scan the lesson to choose the activities and determine the supplies.

Celebration!

This lesson is an optional celebration to mark the accomplishment of learning all the lowercase A-Z phonograms. This marks a significant step in the journey of learning to read and spell in English. Celebrating is not only fun, it helps children to enjoy their accomplishment. We encourage teachers and parents to highlight this achievement with an Alphabet Party. You may choose to celebrate either before or after Review Lesson H.

There are a number of ideas included below.

FOOD: Alphabet pasta, cupcakes with letters, sandwiches cut into letter shapes. Have an A-Z potluck. Assign students a phonogram. They must bring a food that begins with the phonogram to share. Label each dish with the initial phonogram.

CARNIVAL IDEAS: Set the party up like a carnival with phonogram stations. At each station include activities that begin with a particular phonogram. For example for "f" set up a fishing pond. When children catch a fish, they can win fruit, or a flower. For "c", race toy cars down a ramp.

GAMES: Let the students chose their favorite phonogram and reading games to play for prizes.

CRAFTS: Choose a few craft ideas to represent various phonograms. For example for "p" make puppets out of paper bags. Decorate phonogram T-shirts, make an ABC book, ask the students to write each phonogram and draw pictures of words that start with the phonogram.

REVIEW LESSON H

Area	Skill	Mastery
Phonemic Awareness	Distinguish short and long vowel sounds.	3
	Blend two consonants.	2
Handwriting	Write b, h, k, f, v.	1
	Write x, y, z.	2
Phonograms	Read b, h, k, f, v.	1
	Read x, y, z.	2
Reading	Read CVC words.	2
	Read High Frequency CVC words.	1
	Read one-syllable words with consonant blends.	2

Phonemic Awareness Assessment

Short and Long Vowels

H.1 Short and Long Vowel Sounds

I will read a vowel sound. Put your finger on it. Then follow my instruction.

/ĕ/, short /ĕ/. Circle short /ĕ/.
/ā/, long /ā/. Underline long /ā/.
/ĭ/, short /ĭ/. Put an X on short /ĭ/.

Teacher Tip

Alternatively, ask the student to read each of the sounds.

Handwriting Assessment

Handwriting

H.2 Handwriting

Choose the line size that you prefer. Write one of each phonogram.

Multi-Sensory Fun

If the student is not ready to write on paper, show the student the Phonogram Card and have him write the phonogram on a whiteboard or in a sensory box.

Phonogram Assessment

What's That Phonogram?

H.3 What's That Phonogram?

On your page are groups of four phonograms. I will say a sound. Color the phonogram with your highlighter.

1. /b/
2. /f/
3. /h/
4. /k/
5. /v/
6. /x/
7. /y-ĭ-ī-ē/
8. /z/

Highlighter
Phonogram Cards
b, h, k, f, v, x, y, z

Challenge

The ideal handwriting and phonogram assessment would be to dictate the phonogram sound(s) for the student to write on a whiteboard or on paper without a visual reference. These phonograms may be considered mastered.

Phonogram Assessment

Ask the student to read each of the following phonogram cards: b, h, k, f, v, x, y, z

Reading Assessment

Reading

H.4 Reading

Read the phrase. Match it to the picture.

Teacher Tip

The first page includes only CVC words. The second page includes blends. Listen to the student read samples from both pages.

Practice Ideas

Short and Long Vowels

This is a new concept and does not need to be mastered at this time. If the student was uncertain in the assessment, review by showing the Phonogram Cards a, e, i, o, and u and discussing how the first sound is called the short sound and the second sound is called the long sound.

Handwriting

Reteach how to write any of the phonograms that are difficult using the Tactile Cards. Break down each step and have the student repeat the short, bold directions aloud.

"Blind Writing" on page 137
"Word Quilt" on page 157
"The Phonogram Circuit" on page 163
"Run 'n' Match" on page 167
"Phonogram Obstacle Course" on page 203

Teacher Tip

Students who struggle with handwriting should practice writing using large motor movements. It is also beneficial for these students to recite the bold, rhythmic directions aloud when writing.

Phonograms

"Phonogram Kangaroo" on page 173
"Go Fish" on page 181
"Teacher Trouble" on page 190
"Phonogram Snatch" on page 194
"Phonogram Board Game" on page 200

Reading Words

"Act it Out" on page 114
"Read and Do" on page 143
"Reading Basketball" on page 164
"Charades" on page 182
"High Frequency Word Run" on page 191
"High Frequency Word Maze" on page 201

Reading Blends

"Blending Practice" on page 174
"Blending Practice 2" on page 178

Teacher Tip

At this point the student should be able to sound out CVC words. He does not need to read fluently. That will develop with time. Many students will continue to struggle with consonant blends at this stage. Daily practice over time will help students to master this skill. Students may progress to Level B without mastering Consonant Blending.

Index

R

S

V